D0216029

Bloom's

GUIDES

Geoffrey Chaucer's
The Canterbury Tales

The Adventures of Huckleberry Finn
All Quiet on the Western Front
All the Pretty Horses
Animal Farm
The Autobiography of Malcolm X
The Awakening
Beloved
Beowulf
Brave New World
The Canterbury Tales
The Catcher in the Rye
The Chosen
The Crucible
Cry, the Beloved Country
Death of a Salesman
Fahrenheit 451
Frankenstein
The Glass Menagerie
The Grapes of Wrath
Great Expectations
The Great Gatsby
Hamlet
The Handmaid's Tale
The House on Mango Street
I Know Why the Caged Bird Sings
The Iliad
Invisible Man
Jane Eyre

Lord of the Flies
Macbeth
Maggie: A Girl of the Streets
The Member of the Wedding
The Metamorphosis
Native Son
1984
The Odyssey
Oedipus Rex
Of Mice and Men
One Hundred Years of Solitude
Pride and Prejudice
Ragtime
The Red Badge of Courage
Romeo and Juliet
The Scarlet Letter
A Separate Peace
Slaughterhouse-Five
Snow Falling on Cedars
The Stranger
A Streetcar Named Desire
The Sun Also Rises
A Tale of Two Cities
The Things They Carried
To Kill a Mockingbird
Uncle Tom's Cabin
The Waste Land
Wuthering Heights

Bloom's

GUIDES

Geoffrey Chaucer's
The Canterbury Tales

Edited & with an Introduction
by Harold Bloom

BLOOM'S
LITERARY CRITICISM
An imprint of Infobase Publishing

Bloom's Guides: The Canterbury Tales

Copyright © 2008 by Infobase Publishing

Introduction © 2008 by Harold Bloom

Bloom's Literary Criticism
An imprint of Infobase Publishing
132 West 31st Street
New York, NY 10001

Library of Congress Cataloging-in-Publication Data
Geoffrey Chaucer's The Canterbury tales / [edited & with an introduction by] Harold Bloom.
    p. cm. — (Bloom's guides)
  Includes bibliographical references and index.
  ISBN 978-0-7910-9792-2 (hardcover)
    1. Chaucer, Geoffrey, d. 1400. Canterbury tales. 2. Tales, Medieval—History and criticism. I. Bloom, Harold. II. Title: Canterbury tales.

  PR1874.G455 2008
  821'.1—dc22
                        2007048753

You can find Bloom's Literary Criticism on the World Wide Web at
http://www.chelseahouse.com

Contributing Editor: Portia Williams Weiskel
Cover design by Takeshi Takahashi
Printed in the United States of America
Bang EJB 10 9 8 7 6 5 4 3 2 1
This book is printed on acid-free paper.

All links and Web addresses were checked and verified to be correct at the time of publication. Because of the dynamic nature of the Web, some addresses and links may have changed since publication and may no longer be valid.

Contents

Introduction	7
Biographical Sketch	15
The Story Behind the Story	19
List of Characters	23
Summary and Analysis	34
Critical Views	68
G.K. Chesterton on Chaucer's Greatness	68
Arthur W. Hoffman on the Opening Lines of the Prologue	70
E.T. Donaldson on Chaucer the Poet and Pilgrim	72
Paul G. Ruggiers on Chaucerian Comedy	74
V.A. Kolve on Chaucer's Fabliaux	78
Alcuin Blamires on Excess and Restraint in the *Tales*	80
Winthrop Wetherbee on the Absence of Order	82
Anne Laskaya on Chaucer and Competition	84
Derek Brewer on the Miller's Tale	87
Helen Phillips on Intentional Diversity in the *Tales*	89
John C. Hirsh on Love and Death in the Knight's Tale	91
C. David Benson on the First Two Tales	94
Seth Lerer on the Philosophical Question of the *Tales*	96
Lee Patterson on Chaucer as Creator of English Tradition	97
Works by Geoffrey Chaucer	101
Annotated Bibliography	102
Contributors	109
Acknowledgments	112
Index	115

 Introduction

HAROLD BLOOM

I

Chaucer is one of those great writers who defeat almost all criticism, an attribute he shares with Shakespeare, Cervantes, and Tolstoy. There are writers of similar magnitude—Dante, Milton, Wordsworth, Proust—who provoke inspired commentary (amidst much more that is humdrum) but Chaucer, like his few peers, has such mimetic force that the critic is disarmed, and so is left either with nothing or with everything still to do. Much criticism devoted to Chaucer is merely historical, or even theological, as though Chaucer ought to be read as a supreme version of medieval Christianity. But I myself am not a Chaucer scholar, and so I write this only as a general critic of literature and as a common reader of Chaucer.

Together with Shakespeare and a handful of the greater novelists in English, Chaucer carries the language further into unthinkable triumphs of the representation of reality than ought to be possible. The Pardoner and the Wife of Bath, like Hamlet and Falstaff, call into question nearly every mode of criticism that is now fashionable. What sense does it make to speak of the Pardoner or the Wife of Bath as being only a structure of tropes, or to say that any tale they tell has suspended its referential aspect almost entirely? The most Chaucerian and best of all Chaucer critics, E. Talbot Donaldson, remarks of the General Prologue to the *Canterbury Tales* that:

> The extraordinary quality of the portraits is their vitality, the illusion that each gives the reader that the character being described is not a fiction but a person, so that it seems as if the poet has not created but merely recorded.

As a critical remark, this is the indispensable starting-point for reading Chaucer, but contemporary modes of interpretation deny that such an illusion of vitality has any value. Many years ago, I walked through a park in Frankfurt, West Germany, with a good friend who is a leading French theorist of interpretation. I had been in Frankfurt to lecture on Freud; my friend had just arrived to give a talk on Joyce's *Ulysses*. As we walked, I remarked that Joyce's Leopold Bloom seemed to me the most sympathetic and affectionate person I had encountered in any fiction. My friend, annoyed and perplexed, replied that Poldy was *not* a person and that my statement therefore was devoid of sense. Though not agreeing, I reflected silently that the difference between my friend and myself could not be reconciled by anything I could say. To him, *Ulysses* was not even persuasive rhetoric, but was a system of tropes. To me, it was above all else the personality of Poldy. My friend's deconstructionism, I again realized, was only another formalism, a very tough-minded and skeptical formalism. But all critical formalism reaches its limits rather quickly when fictions are strong enough. L.C. Knights famously insisted that Lady Macbeth's children were as meaningless a critical issue as the girlhood of Shakespeare's heroines, a view in which Knights followed E.E. Stoll who, whether he knew it or not, followed E.A. Poe. To Knights, Falstaff "is not a man, but a choric commentary." The paradox, though, is that this "choric commentary" is more vital than we are, which teaches us that Falstaff is neither trope nor commentary, but a representation of what a human being *might* be, if that person were even wittier than Oscar Wilde, and even more turbulently high-spirited than Zero Mostel. Falstaff, Poldy, the Wife of Bath: these are what Shelley called "forms more real than living man."

Immensely original authors (and they are not many) seem to have no precursors, and so seem to be children without parents. Shakespeare is the overwhelming instance, since he swallowed up his immediate precursor Christopher Marlowe, whereas Chaucer charmingly claims fictive authorities while being immensely indebted to actual French and Italian writers and to Boccaccio in particular. Yet it may be that Chaucer is as much Shakespeare's great original as he was Spenser's. What is virtually without precedent in Shakespeare is that his characters *change themselves by pondering upon what they themselves say*. In Homer and the Bible and Dante, we do not find sea-changes in particular persons brought about by those persons' own language, that is, by the differences that individual diction and tone make as speech produces further speech. But the Pardoner and the Wife of Bath are well along the mimetic way that leads to Hamlet and Falstaff. What they say to others, and to themselves, partly reflects what they already are, but partly engenders also what they will be. And perhaps even more subtly and forcefully, Chaucer suggests ineluctable transformations going on in the Pardoner and the Wife of Bath through the effect of the language of the tales they choose to tell.

Something of this shared power in Chaucer and Shakespeare accounts for the failures of criticism to apprehend them, particularly when criticism is formalist, or too given over to the study of codes, conventions, and what is now called "language" but might more aptly be called applied linguistics, or even psycholinguistics. A critic addicted to what is now called the "priority of language over meaning" will not be much given to searching for meaning in persons, real or imagined. But persons, at once real *and* imagined, are the fundamental basis of the experiential art of Chaucer and Shakespeare. Chaucer and Shakespeare know, beyond knowing, the labyrinthine ways in which the individual self is always a picnic of selves. "The poets were there before me," Freud remarked, and perhaps Nietzsche ought to have remarked the same.

II

Talbot Donaldson rightly insists, against the patristic exegetes, that Chaucer was primarily a comic writer. This need never be qualified, if we also judge the Shakespeare of the two parts of *Henry IV* to be an essentially comic writer, as well as Fielding, Dickens, and Joyce. "Comic writer" here means something very comprehensive, with the kind of "comedy" involved being more in the mode, say, of Balzac than that of Dante, deeply as Chaucer was indebted to Dante notwithstanding. If the Pardoner is fundamentally a comic figure, why, then, so is Vautrin? Balzac's hallucinatory "realism," a cosmos in which every janitor is a genius, as Baudelaire remarked, has its affinities with the charged vitalism of Chaucer's fictive world. The most illuminating exegete of the General Prologue to the *Canterbury Tales* remains William Blake, whose affinities with Chaucer were profound. This is the Blake classed by Yeats, in *A Vision*, with Rabelais and Aretino; Blake as an heroic vitalist whose motto was "Exuberance is Beauty," which is an apt Chaucerian slogan also. I will grant that the Pardoner's is a negative exuberance, and yet Blake's remarks show us that the Wife of Bath's exuberance has its negative aspects also.

Comic writing so large and so profound hardly seems to admit a rule for literary criticism. Confronted by the Wife of Bath or Falstaff or the suprahuman Poldy, how shall the critic conceive her or his enterprise? What is there left to be done? I grimace to think of the Wife of Bath and Falstaff deconstructed, or of having their life-augmenting contradictions subjected to a Marxist critique. The Wife of Bath and difference (or even "differance")? Falstaff and surplus value? Poldy and the dogma that there is nothing outside the text? Hamlet and Lacan's Mirror Phase? The heroic, the vitalizing pathos of a fully human vision, brought about through a supermimesis not of essential nature, but of human possibility, demands a criticism more commensurate with its scope and its color. It is a matter of aesthetic tact, certainly, but as Oscar Wilde taught us, that makes it truly a moral matter as well. What devitalizes the Wife of Bath, or Falstaff, or Poldy, tends at last to reduce us also.

III

That a tradition of major poetry goes from Chaucer to Spenser and Milton and on through them to Blake and Wordsworth, Shelley and Keats, Browning and Tennyson and Whitman, Yeats and Stevens, D.H. Lawrence and Hart Crane, is now widely accepted as a critical truth. The myth of a metaphysical countertradition, from Donne and Marvell through Dryden, Pope, and Byron on to Hopkins, Eliot, and Pound, has been dispelled and seen as the Eliotic invention it truly was. Shakespeare is too large for any tradition, and so is Chaucer. One can wonder if even the greatest novelists in the language—Richardson, Austen, George Eliot, Dickens, Henry James, and the Mark Twain of *Huckleberry Finn* (the one true rival of *Moby-Dick* and *Leaves of Grass* as *the* American book or Bible), or Conrad, Lawrence, and Faulkner in this century—can approach Shakespeare and Chaucer in the astonishing art of somehow creating fictions that are more human than we generally are. Criticism, perhaps permanently ruined by Aristotle's formalism, has had little hope of even accurately describing this art. Aristophanes, Plato, and Longinus are apter models for a criticism more adequate to Chaucer and to Shakespeare. Attacking Euripides, Aristophanes, as it were, attacks Chaucer and Shakespeare in a true prolepsis, and Plato's war against Homer, his attack upon mimesis, prophesies an unwaged war upon Chaucer and Shakespeare. Homer and Euripides, after all, simply are not the mimetic scandal that is constituted by Chaucer and Shakespeare; the *inwardness* of the Pardoner and Hamlet is of a different order from that of Achilles and Medea. Freud himself does not catch up to Chaucer and Shakespeare; he gets as far as Montaigne and Rousseau, which indeed is a long journey into the interior. But the Pardoner is the interior and even Iago, even Goneril and Regan, Cornwall and Edmund, do not give us a fiercer sense of intolerable resonance on the way down and out. Donaldson subtly observes that "it is the Pardoner's particular tragedy that, except in church, every one can see through him at a glance." The profound phrase here is "except in church." What happens to, or better yet, *within* the Pardoner when he preaches in church? Is that not parallel to asking what happens within the dying Edmund when he murmurs, "Yet Edmund was beloved," and thus somehow is moved to make his belated, futile attempt to save Cordelia and Lear? Are there any critical codes or methods that could possibly help us to sort out the Pardoner's more-than-Dostoevskian intermixture of supernatural faith and preternatural chicanery? Will semiotics or even Lacanian psycholinguistics anatomize Edmund for us, let alone Regan?

Either we become experiential critics when we read Chaucer and Shakespeare, or in too clear a sense we never read them at all. "Experiential" here necessarily means humane observation both of others and of ourselves, which leads to testing such observations in every context that indisputably is relevant. Longinus is the ancestor of such experiential criticism, but its masters are Samuel Johnson, Hazlitt and Emerson, Ruskin, Pater, and Wilde. A century gone mad on method has given us no critics to match these, nor are they likely to come again soon, though we still have Northrop Frye and Kenneth Burke, their last legitimate descendants.

IV

Mad on method, we have turned to rhetoric, and so much so that the best of us, the late Paul de Man, all but urged us to identify literature with rhetoric, so that criticism perhaps would become again the rhetoric of rhetoric, rather than a Burkean rhetoric of motives or a Fryean rhetoric of desires. Expounding the Nun's Priest's Tale, Talbot Donaldson points to "the enormous rhetorical elaboration of the telling" and is moved to a powerful insight into experiential criticism:

Rhetoric here is regarded as the inadequate defense that mankind erects against an inscrutable reality; rhetoric enables man at best to regard himself as a being of heroic proportions—like Achilles, or like Chauntecleer—and at worst to maintain the last sad vestiges of his dignity (as a rooster Chauntecleer is carried in the fox's mouth, but as a hero he rides on his back), rhetoric enables man to find significance both in his desires and in his fate, and to pretend to himself that the universe takes him seriously. And rhetoric has a habit, too, of collapsing in the presence of simple common sense.

12

Yet rhetoric, as Donaldson implies, if it is Chaucer's rhetoric in particular, can be a life-enhancing as well as a life-protecting defense. Here is the heroic pathos of the Wife of Bath, enlarging existence even as she sums up its costs in one of those famous Chaucerian passages that herald Shakespearean exuberances to come:

> But Lord Crist, whan that it remembreth me
> Upon my youthe and on my jolitee,
> It tikleth me aboute myn herte roote—
> Unto this day it dooth myn herte boote
> That I have had my world as in my time.
> But age, allas, that al wol envenime,
> Hath me biraft my beautee and my pith—
> Lat go, farewel, the devel go therwith!
> The flour is goon, ther is namore to telle:
> The bren as I best can now moste I selle;
> But yit to be right merye wol I fonde.
> (*WBP*, 1.475; E.T. Donaldson, 2d ed.)

The defense against time, so celebrated as a defiance of time's revenges, is the Wife's fierce assertion also of the will to live at whatever expense. Rhetorically, the center of the passage is in the famously immense reverberation of her great cry of exultation and loss, "That I have had my world as in my time," where the double "my" is decisive, yet the "have had" falls away in a further intimation of mortality. Like Falstaff, the Wife is a grand trope of pathos, of life defending itself against every convention that would throw us into death-in-life. Donaldson wisely warns us that "pathos, however, must not be allowed to carry the day," and points to the coarse vigor of the Wife's final benediction to the tale she has told:

> And Jesu Crist us sende
> Housbondes meeke, yonge, and fresshe abedde—
> And grace t'overbide hem that we wedde.

And eek I praye Jesu shorte hir lives
That nought wol be governed by hir wives,
And olde and angry nigardes of dispence—
God sende hem soone a verray pestilence!
(*WBT*, 1. 402)

Blake feared the Wife of Bath because he saw in her what he called the Female Will incarnate. By the Female Will, Blake meant the will of the natural woman or the natural man, a prolepsis perhaps of Schopenhauer's rapacious Will to Live or Freud's "frontier concept" of the drive. Chaucer, I think, would not have quarreled with such an interpretation, but he would have scorned Blake's dread of the natural will or Schopenhauer's horror of its rapacity. Despite every attempt to assimilate him to a poetry of belief, Chaucer actually surpasses even Shakespeare as a celebrant of the natural heart, while like Shakespeare being beyond illusions concerning the merely natural. No great poet was less of a dualist than Chaucer was, and nothing makes poetry more difficult for critics, because all criticism is necessarily dualistic.

The consolation for critics and readers is that Chaucer and Shakespeare, Cervantes and Tolstoy, persuade us finally that everything remains to be done in the development of a criticism dynamic and comprehensive enough to represent such absolute writers without reduction or distortion. No codes or methods will advance the reading of Chaucer. The critic is thrown back upon herself or himself, and upon the necessity to become a vitalizing interpreter in the service of an art whose burden is only to carry more life forward into a time without boundaries.

Biographical Sketch

Biographies of ancient and medieval peoples are difficult to develop because no concept of human personality—or perceived value in documenting it—comparable to our own, existed at the time. Because Chaucer came to occupy a singular place in the history of world literature, much painstaking labor has gone into establishing a picture of his life, but some details are still in the realm of informed speculation. There are two Chaucers, even a third. The first is the public man about whom official records give a significant accounting. Only because Chaucer had employment at the court do we have any information.

Born in the early 1340s to a successful wine merchant, John Chaucer, and his wife, Agnes de Copton, said to be related to an official at the British Mint, young Chaucer began his life in the relatively secure and prosperous middle class of London. His life was not secure from every threat, though. When Chaucer was a child, a rat hosting a flea carrying the bacterium responsible for the Black Plague traveled on a ship from France to Dorset in England in 1348, and nearly a third of the population died. Chaucer and his family escaped the wave of illness and death, most likely because the family had the means to stay in Southampton, away from the dirty and densely populated city of London. Chaucer made one reference to the plague, in his Pardoner's Tale.

The plague might also explain why no public records account for the unusually broad learning evident in his writing. According to one biographer (Peter Ackroyd, *Chaucer*, 2004), Chaucer's parents could have afforded private tutors, and Chaucer may have intermittently attended nearby St. Paul's School where he possibly received instruction in Latin and French, Ovid and Virgil.

The first mention of Chaucer appears in the accounting records for the household of the countess of Ulster, who became the wife of Lionel, third son of Edward III, the reigning king of England. The scarcity of biographical details is illustrated by the date of this discovery. Scholars and handwriting experts examining manuscripts acquired by the British Museum in 1851 found a notation indicating that a certain Geoffrey Chaucer received two shillings, six pence to purchase the appropriate outfit for a page: a short jacket, shoes, and red and black leg wear.

Pages were young boys between ten and seventeen. Their duties were mundane—making beds, waiting on the tables and whims of the noble family—but the job was also an opportunity to learn manners and be exposed to people from a variety of backgrounds. Another biographer (D.S. Brewer, *Chaucer*, third edition, 1973) speculates that in the company of older pageboys, Chaucer would have been privy to gossip about palace life. Listening and observing might have been entertaining distractions for pageboys as well as skills Chaucer would hone and later put to good use. There was also the possibility for advancement. Fortuitously, Chaucer later served as page for the duke of Lancaster (John of Gaunt) who became both his patron and protector.

The main biographical questions about Chaucer concern how he became clever enough to imagine and write the *Canterbury Tales* and how he became familiar with the range of characters that populate and narrate them. His pageboy employment was one influence, but life in London must have been a primary education in itself. Medieval London was a vibrant and productive city of 50,000 people. The Chaucer family house on Thames Street was close to the docks, where goods came and went and where merchants sold wares in street stalls. Farm animals roamed the streets along with bakers and field workers bringing in bread and produce. Nearby was the Steelyard, quarters for German workers, and a colony of Genoese merchants. Bells announcing Mass and religious pageants were constant features: there were ninety-nine churches in London at the time. Mystery plays enacted on the streets juxtaposed religious themes with boisterous farce and obscenities. There were violent spectacles as well: cockfighting, wild boars fighting to the death, dogs attacking defanged bears. And nearby was the site for the public hanging of criminals.

With an inquisitive spirit, Chaucer could have had the best possible education just by being exposed to and growing up among the streets of London. As he entered adulthood, he was developing into a poet famous for his amazing characters and their fabulous stories. The material for an inventive person was at hand.

Chaucer spent his lifetime as a well-respected public servant. He participated in campaigns during the Hundred Years War, was captured in France and ransomed for a sum to which Edward III personally contributed. In 1366 he married Philippi de Roet, a lady-in-waiting in the court. There was at least one child, Thomas. Apparently Chaucer had a low opinion of marriage; after his wife died, in approximately 1387, he wrote a poem stating he would never "to falle of weddynge in the trappe." In 1368 Chaucer began traveling as the king's emissary to France and Italy. Already multilingual, Chaucer learned Italian, and scholars speculate that his sojourns in Italy may have acquainted him with Boccaccio and his *Decameron*. In 1374 Chaucer was appointed controller of customs at the port of London—an important position—and continued to travel abroad, entrusted with diplomatic missions. In 1380 Chaucer survived a scandal: he was cleared of charges of rape. He went on to serve briefly as a Member of Parliament from 1385 to 1386.

Chaucer was intermittently employed for the remainder of his life, but after the death of Edward III and the accession of Richard II (1377), he lost some of his responsibilities. It was during these last years that he became the second Chaucer—author and poet—and made a different use of his impressively broad education. Along with the Latin writers, Chaucer had read Dante and Boccaccio. He had been introduced to the tradition of courtly love through his experiences at the French courts. Today he would be called an intellectual and a philosopher as well as a poet. His eclectic interests are demonstrated by his translations: a thirteenth-century French romance *Roman de la Rose*; a treatise on astronomy; and *The Consolation of Philosophy*, a treatise on free will and human destiny by the Roman philosopher Boethius. This diversity of interests also shows up in the *Canterbury Tales*. Between 1380 and 1387 Chaucer wrote *The House of Fame*, *The Parliament of Fowls*, *Troilus and Criseyde*, and *The Legend of Good Women*. He began work on the *Tales* in 1380 and continued until he died, leaving a great but incomplete work.

The *Canterbury Tales* was popular, and illustrations of Chaucer reading them aloud to different audiences are often included in biographies and books of critical commentary. He had created his own third identity: as one of the pilgrims on the way to Canterbury. Much speculation has been focused on Chaucer's personality—as pilgrim and historical figure. Scholars concur there is some overlap. Chaucer the author permits some references to his physical appearance: short, stout, ruddy, and bearded. His personality comes through his poetry and is consistent with what has been surmised from his employment history. In the words of another Chaucer scholar:

> Every reader [of the *Tales*] feels that he is in the presence of a genial and urbane man, endlessly intrigued by the life about him, interested in people of all kinds, amused at their foibles and weaknesses, tolerant outwardly even of the vicious.
> (Beryl Rowland, ed., *Companion to Chaucer Studies*, Oxford University Press, 1968, 11)

Chaucer's last known home was a small house with a garden in the quiet township of Westminster. He died in 1400 and was buried in Westminster Abbey, the first in what is now known as the Poets' Corner.

The Story Behind the Story

Readers of the *Canterbury Tales* may already know about Chaucer's unique cast of characters but not the singular position Chaucer and his *Tales* occupy in the history of English literature. Chaucer was the first English person to be known as an "author." A summary of his life in Thomas Speght's 1598 edition of the *Tales* is the first biography written in English about an English writer. Chaucer's lifetime coincided with the return of English as the official language of England. The nation's earliest literature—Caedmon's *Hymn* (c. 658) and *Beowulf* (anonymous, eighth century)—was written in Old English (Anglo-Saxon). After the Norman Conquest in 1066, French (or a version often referred to as Anglo-Norman) supplanted English as the language of the ruling aristocracy. Chaucer's various business transactions were conducted in French, but he spoke in the Middle English dialect of London (the forerunner to modern standard and American English). As the Norman influence waned, English was reinstated, invigorated by an infusion of English vernacular and eloquent court rhetoric. With his broad education and knowledge of languages, Chaucer was both a beneficiary of and contributor to this evolution of the English language.

"That Chaucer is the founding figure of the English literature tradition is not really in doubt. But the interesting question is not *whether* but *why*," writes Chaucer scholar Lee Patterson (*Geoffrey Chaucer's "The Canterbury Tales*," 2007, p. 5). One explanation, Patterson argues, is that Chaucer believed England was capable of creating a national literature:

> [The *Canterbury Tales*] . . . is a compilation of almost every kind of writing known to the Middle Ages. Epic, romance, fabliau, saint's life, exemplum, sermon, mirror of princes, penitential treatise, tragedy, animal fable, Breton lay, confessional autobiography, Marian miracle—all these and more are present. . . . Each of the genres . . . invokes

not just specific writers but a whole lexicon of different kinds of writing (7).

Seventeenth-century poet John Dryden had another explanation for Chaucer's status, also related to the *Tales*:

[Chaucer] has taken into the compass of his *Canterbury Tales* the various manners and humors (as we now call them) of the whole English nation in his age. Not a single character has escaped him. All his pilgrims are severally distinguished from each other; and not only in their inclinations but in their very physiognomies and persons. . . . Even the ribaldry of the low characters is different: the Reeve, the Miller, and the Cook are . . . distinguished from each other as much as the mincing Lady Prioress and the broad-speaking, gap-toothed Wife of Bath. . . . [There] is such a variety. . . . [Here] is God's plenty.
(*Preface to Fables Ancient and Modern*, 1700)

Chaucer's pilgrims are realistic (although not practical in the contemporary sense); they interact in convincing ways; and some gain self-understanding as a consequence of the pilgrimage. Notably, Chaucer's *Tales* mark the first occasion in literature where everyday activities are the main subject.

Chaucer began writing the *Tales* in 1386 and continued until his death in 1400. He lived for a time in Greenwich along the pilgrimage route between London and Canterbury, and it is easy to imagine that inspiration for the *Tales* came from watching the continual stream of travelers outside his window. The shrine of Thomas à Becket is located in the Canterbury Cathedral near the spot where he was murdered in 1170 by soldiers acting on orders from King Henry II. The site became a favorite destination for pilgrims after the archbishop's blood was discovered to have healing powers.

"[Chaucer] finished his own pilgrimage before he finished his pilgrims'," another critic has stated (Hallissy, 6). Numerous tales were originally planned—four for each of thirty pilgrims, two on the way and two on the way back. At his death only the

Prologue and twenty-four tales (two incomplete) were written. More than eighty manuscripts of the *Tales* exist, all compiled after Chaucer's death and all arranged in a different order. The commonly used Ellesmere Manuscript promotes interest in the individuality of the pilgrims by including sketches of each.

The pilgrims' stories reflect the values and conflicts that animated Chaucer's century. Church and state were competing authorities, and their representatives tell different kinds of stories. The Peasants' Revolution of 1381 was partially triggered by the growing disparity among the classes as well as by resentments between "townies" and students. Transitions between reigning powers were filled with strife, even regicide. These are the years Shakespeare dramatized in his King Henry plays. (There is evidence that Chaucer was acquainted with the Prince Hal of those plays, who became Henry IV.) Fear of fate's capricious power to reverse one's fortune was symbolized by the goddess Fortuna with her wheel. Christianity, in contrast, provided a difficult but reassuring principle of order by conceptualizing life as a mysterious journey—a pilgrimage— to God. The notion of a First Mover—the energy that sets in motion everything in the universe—was (and still is) an ongoing preoccupation. Salvation came through adherence to Church teachings. Medieval women were revered (as Mary and maternal figures) and maligned (as Eve figures, capable of causing the downfall of God's creation). The feudal system equated women with property; instruction books on appropriate behavior were written for wives. The Wife of Bath, Griselda, Alisoun, Constance, and the Prioress represent these diverse images.

Without the yet-to-be-invented printing press, books were handmade and rare. Chaucer's stories were well suited for reading aloud. They are full of surprises and odd juxtapositions. Interconnected but able to stand alone, they are about familiar and colorful people who display a range of emotions and conflicts. Many of their commentaries and odd predicaments cause readers to laugh out loud.

The *Canterbury Tales* has been especially prized for its great comic spirit, but not always for its salacious details. *Troilus and*

Criseyde (c. 1385) was regarded as Chaucer's greatest achievement by both the Romantics and the Victorians. The *Tales*, according to scholar John H. Fisher, was "known and deplored" by clerics and defenders of Elizabethan high culture: ". . . a 'Canterbury tale' [was] a term for something vulgar and demeaning" (Fisher, 157). Dryden's comments (quoted above) shifted the focus from "moralizing" to appreciating Chaucer's innovative uses of drama and narrative and the remarkable "lifelikeness" of his characters. Many of Shakespeare's characters were ribald, but among his contemporaries, some were shocked by Chaucer. In his book on the subject, Professor Thomas W. Ross asserts that "Chaucer uses risqué words for one major purpose: to delineate comic characters and thus to make us laugh" (Ross, 1). Citing other scholars on Chaucer's use of puns, Ross argues that the device allowed Chaucer to give words multiple meaning and thus to say more than one thing at a time. Ross reminds us that Chaucer is responsible for his characters' words, despite his protestations to the contrary, and one pleasure of reading him is discovering the poet's different personas: "[Chaucer's] customary trick is to claim he is simply reporting others' words: the drunken Miller is a 'cherl,' as everybody knows. *He* said those words—not *I*, Geoffrey Chaucer" (2).

Through the years, many scholars have enjoyed writing about Chaucer's humor. British essayist G.K. Chesterton said Chaucer's greatest virtue ". . . is something that neither Puritanism nor the Public School has contrived to kill; he is generally fond of a joke. His great national contribution to Christendom . . . is the English sense of humour" (Chesterton, 197). He concludes:

> [Chaucer] makes fun of people, in the exact sense of getting fun out of them for himself. He does not make game of them, in the actual sense of hunting them down and killing them like . . . public pests. He does not want the Friar and the Wife of Bath to perish; one would sometimes suspect that he does not really want them to change. (199)

List of Characters

Many readers find Chaucer's pilgrims and their relationships as entertaining and instructive as their tales. New readers unfamiliar with Chaucer's times may find these character portraits a lively and compelling way to get a sense of life in medieval England. Scholars of this period emphasize the importance that hierarchy—both social and ecclesiastical—had on the people and their daily lives. Chaucer attempts (not always successfully) to establish and maintain a recognizable order for his pilgrims. Disruptions of that order tell much about the social turbulence of his time.

For clarity, in the following descriptions, Pilgrim Chaucer is "the narrator," and Poet Chaucer is "Chaucer." The difference in their perspectives is more than half the fun and interest in the *Tales*.

The **Knight** is the first pilgrim to be described and the first to relate a tale. "Chance" is the reason given, but Chaucer reserves the honored position for the Knight because the chivalrous figure carried the most authority in medieval society and served both secular and religious ideals. This particular knight is idealized; his perfection is the measure for all who follow. It is, however, unlikely that a single knight in a single lifetime could have fought all the battles attributed to him. And at least one of those battles was not a holy war fought in defense of Christendom, so perhaps he took a few mercenary excursions. Is it excessive zeal, a lack of planning, or forgetfulness that explains why the Knight shows up for the pilgrimage in his battle-stained armor?

The **Squire**, the curly-headed son of the Knight and a youthful version of him, has plenty of zeal but lacks the discipline he will need. The narrator refers to him as a "lad of fire"; he is so preoccupied with his lady-love that "he slept as little as a nightingale."

Traveling as a servant to both the Knight and the Squire is the green and brown **Yeoman**. After decking him out with woodsman's clothes and a hunter's bow, the narrator appears to be playing the naïf here when he states the obvious: "He was a proper forester, I guess." The Yeoman's longbow was a new weapon in Chaucer's lifetime.

The **Prioress** is the first of Chaucer's religious figures and the first to be identified as an individual (she has her own name): her personality is marked by its striking contradictions. She must have caught the narrator's attention early; he observed her long enough to notice her oddly perfect table manners: ". . . not a morsel from her lips did she let fall." "Over-refined" describes the Prioress: she "[strains] to counterfeit a courtly kind of grace . . . [one that is] fitting to her place." Her affections appear unbalanced: she swoons over an injured mouse but not apparently for poor people. Her spoiled little dogs also get more of her devotion than God. The leftovers from a convent kitchen are given to her coddled pets instead of to the local poor. The inscription in her bright golden brooch—*Amor vincit omnia*, Love conquers all—brings into question the kind of love—sacred or profane, of God or of man—she is keeping close to her heart. Another quality that is commonly not associated with a nun is the Prioress's apparent preoccupation with social position and appearance—concerns more appropriate for a lady of the court. Contemporary audiences probably find the Prioress inoffensively pretentious. Chaucer's satire focuses on the discrepancies in her self-perception.

The **Monk**, second of the religious figures, is an odd man who has rejected the monastic life: "[The text that scorns] a monk out of his cloister . . . was a text he held not worth an oyster." Not only is he not a humble figure associated with the ascetic life of prayer, fasting, and service, this monk is impressively robust, like his horses, and adamant in his resistance to St. Augustine's instruction that monks perform some field labor. The monk's idea of manual labor consists of riding his horses to the hunt and eating heartily afterwards. The narrator is nonetheless quite taken with this "manly" monk; he even uses the monk's own words to defend him: "Why should he study till his head went round poring over books in cloisters?" Where the Prioress had pretensions to piety, the monk has none, and Chaucer has his narrator make this unsubtle observation: "He was a prelate fit for exhibition."

Another religious figure more worldly than pious is the **Friar**. Unlike the Prioress whose worldliness is relatively harmless or the monk whose enthusiasm for worldly pleasures causes no deprivation to others, the Friar's self-justifying story about his various behaviors reveals a corrupt figure at heart. Friars were noncloistered monks. These wandering mendicants took vows of service through holy poverty which many violated, some egregiously. Chaucer's friar exemplifies the institutional corruption that marked the Church of the Middle Ages. The narrator is taken in by the Friar; he calls him a "noble pillar to his Order," but each action ascribed to him violates the sacred duties entrusted to him. Friars were expected to serve the "least among us," in particular the lepers and other outcasts this friar energetically avoids, preferring to cavort with barmaids. His greatest sin is violating the sacrament of hearing confessions. Claiming to have more power to give absolution than the average priest, the Friar attracts more confessors and thus more money: "He was an easy man in penance giving / where he could hope to make a decent living." The Friar is responsible for a double sin: he sells forgiveness, and the sinner does no authentic penance. This dereliction of duty harms his parishioners, and his cleverly rationalized self-deceit gravely harms himself.

The next group of pilgrims is neither religious nor chivalrous. They are professionals, who pursue private gain—the merchant and the lawyer in particular—over service to others.

The nameless **Merchant** serves an essential but narrow purpose in society—trade and commerce. He is "worthy" in the sense that he takes responsibility for a high-stakes venture: battling pirates and capricious weather at sea to bring needed goods to his clients. His deceit is not of himself but of others about himself. Actually in debt, he must appear successful to keep his enterprise going. A motley-dressed anonymous merchant on a pilgrimage could be running away from his creditors, but Chaucer does not know or speculate.

"Clerk" in Chaucer's time referred to someone associated with the ecclesiastical or intellectual life. Chaucer's **Clerk**, an Oxford student, is an austere intellectual; he lives without physical comfort. He is nearly as emaciated as his horse, and his threadbare clothes are more like those the Friar and other servants of God should be arrayed in but are not. The Clerk has no idle speech, no pleasantries—"He never spoke a word more than was need." He is a solitary hardworking soul and perhaps not much fun to be around. He has friends, however. They pay for his books, and he pays them back with prayers. We learn the Clerk is unemployed, but he seems indisposed to do anything except pursue more learning, preferring twenty tomes of Aristotle to fine robes. Unlike the Merchant or the Friar, he has a remarkable disregard for making money. He also possesses no phoniness or hypocrisy, no self-deception or self-seeking ways. He is cheerful: "And gladly would he learn, and gladly teach."

Chaucer's **Man of Law** is disconcertingly similar to the contemporary cynical image of the lawyer. The narrator's conjecture that the Lawyer is not as busy as he likes to appear to be, nor as rich, is an amusing bit of satire about the legal profession. Although Chaucer's lawyer has acquired an extensive legal knowledge—including the stored memory of every legal decision since the time of King William I (1099)—he has used it more frequently to acquire real estate than to administer justice. Like the Merchant and the Friar, the Lawyer is skilled at concealing his self-promoting motives.

The pagan philosopher Epicurus (321–270 B.C.E.) located human happiness in the sensual pleasures, especially those having to do with preparing and eating fine food. By contrast, medieval Christianity was ambivalent about feasting; asceticism was espoused as a method of nourishing the soul, but feast days were celebrated in the Church calendar. No ambivalence about fasting is felt by the **Franklin**, whom the narrator calls "Epicurus' own true son." Chaucer's Franklin happily uses his acquired wealth for gustatory and social pleasures. His hospitality is abundant and always extended; likened to Saint Julian, the patron of hospitality, a lavish table is permanently set in his house. Besides the normal fare served at medieval tables are delicacies of the season revealing an extra measure of attentiveness to food and its elaborate preparation. Despite the Franklin's immersion in materialism, he covets no additional wealth and is neither deceptive nor self-deceiving. His robust coloring and jovial nature suggest a kind of secular Santa Claus.

The **Haberdasher, Carpenter, Weaver, Dyer,** and **Tapestry-maker** are tradesmen belonging to the same guild, an institution similar to a modern trade union. Chaucer's attention to their finely detailed apparel suggests their skill and prosperity as well as their aspirations to occupy a higher social class. Their wives' pretentious behaviors match these aspirations. They wear showy robes and answer to "Madam," as if they were royalty. Chaucer's amusement with human pretensions animates these satirical portraits, but upheavals in the social hierarchy of his time were a reality informing these various portrayals.

The guild brings its own **Cook**—another show of prosperity. The cook is talented, but the ulcer on his leg noted by the narrator makes the thought of eating his meals unappetizing. The narrator's congeniality or naiveté prevents any mention of the disgust or disease associated with unhealed wounds. The satire and revulsion of this scene are experienced wholly by the reader, while the narrator continues merrily on his way.

The **Seaman** behaves like a pirate, but may simply be a merchant mariner who could turn into a rogue without qualms. Chaucer reports only his activity. Out on the high seas, where the seaman forces his conquered enemies to "swim home," a fortune can be made. This skillful scoundrel sails right by us without eliciting any judgment from the narrator.

Why a nonbelieving doctor would join a religious pilgrimage is unclear. But in his colorful attire, advertising his affluence and success, the **Doctor** joins the other travelers. He is exceptionally knowledgeable about medicine and healing—no one alive knows more—and, like contemporary doctors, reveres Hippocrates. The doctor impresses the narrator who must rely on the former's testimony for evidence of his medical successes. Medieval medicine combined the patient's self-reported symptoms with his or her planetary signs to diagnose and treat afflictions. Human health was maintained by a balance of the four elements and humours—earth, air, water, fire; black bile, yellow bile, blood, phlegm. (Interestingly, these primitive-sounding notions of balance remain important in both Eastern and Western paradigms of human health.) The Doctor—were he to read the Bible—would learn that healing should not be related to profit making, but we are told that he regards the plague as a source of income: ". . . he was rather close as to expenses / And kept the gold he won in pestilences." His professional ethics are compromised in other ways as well. He and his accomplice at the Apothecary profit from each other's business.

The flamboyant, formidable, and gap-toothed **Wife of Bath** is in a class by herself. The image of the short, stout, and ruddy Chaucer traveling along with this larger-than-life lady is one of the most memorable in the *Canterbury Tales*. Known internationally for her superior weaving, she is undoubtedly wearing some of her own handiwork. Details of manner and dress identify her as a member of the rising middle class. Strong-willed, she has outlived five husbands and under Church law she would have been entitled to five separate inheritances, making her a rare figure for medieval audiences: an independent woman with the sufficient means to travel alone. Not donning widow's mourning clothes, the Wife of

Bath is dressed up almost in costume with bright colors and an oversized hat. The narrator is charmed by her, perhaps even a bit dazzled. Five husbands, he reports, and then adds, in disbelief, not including all those lovers from her youth that she did not marry! Poignancy mingles with her confident self-assertiveness; although she remains vibrant, she has seen plenty of death and laments her own aging. But nothing stops her from enjoying social chatter, as she injects her lively presence into the group.

By this point, we know enough from the narrator's commentary to see that human failings have not changed much over the centuries. Pride, pretension, and avarice are alive and present in everyone. Meeting the **Parson**, good pilgrim and the first honest practitioner of his sacred duties, reminds us of human decency as well. Humble and holy, the Parson, in Christian imagery, is a hovering shepherd, devoted to each sheep no matter how inconveniently it has strayed from the flock. Chaucer scholar E.T. Donaldson points out that the plague had depopulated entire regions, leaving the parson with greater distances to travel for fewer souls. Many chose to change location for more lucrative assignments, but Chaucer's Parson keeps true to his mission. In integrity, the Parson is kin to the Knight; the only hint of imperfect behavior is his quickness to rebuke anyone who has gone astray. The Parson stands at the opposite end of the ethical spectrum from the Friar, Pardoner, and Summoner, but in contrast to these miscreants, he has no identifying details. He functions more as an ideal, reminding readers, and the other pilgrims, of their manifold failings.

Another virtuous pilgrim is the Parson's brother, the **Plowman**, an honest and hardworking laborer. His is the lowliest work; twice the narrator portrays him hauling manure. This loyal peasant farmer belongs with the blessed meek whom Jesus, in the Beatitudes, says will inherit the earth. Perhaps Chaucer links these good brothers to highlight their different but essential services—the Parson's to the spiritual life of others through attending to their spiritual needs, and the Plowman's to the physical needs for sustaining life on earth as an expression of his Christian duty. Chaucer has framed here an ideal of medieval order and community.

Order is undermined by the five remaining pilgrims, the true "low lifes" of medieval society, scoundrels and cheaters all. Curiously the narrator (in a moment of self-deprecating humor?) places himself among these thugs. The **Miller** is comically grotesque with his hairy wart, flared nostrils, and a mouth as large as a furnace door. For reasons unclear—perhaps because sheer bulk is all he has—the Miller likes to show off by running into large doors and smashing them with his head. He is not without a trade, however; he mills grain and cheats his customers. Nor is he without talent; he plays the bagpipes and leads the group out of town. A dirty joke for a tale can be expected from this character.

Fit company for the Miller is the band of crooks that follows, each one with his own scam. The **Manciple** buys provisions for an organization of lawyers. He pays less for the goods than he gets in reimbursement and pockets the difference. The narrator seems more amused than shocked by the Manciple's cleverness in outwitting his employers.

A reeve serves the lord of an estate. He implements and accounts for the lord's management of his lands and serfs. Chaucer's **Reeve** is another petty crook, an embezzler of sorts, getting as much profit out of the work done by serfs but reporting a lower yield to the lord and keeping the difference. Although he has a spiffy horse and a nice home, the Reeve's dress and demeanor suggest a life devoid of meaning or pleasure. The Reeve is so shameless that he lends money to the lord whom he has stolen it from.

The deceitfulness of the next two pilgrims is especially egregious because each is entrusted with a sacred service to the Church community. Summoners earned their living by summoning to trial all violators of Church laws. Offenses included failure to tithe, committing adultery, or cursing in God's name. Chaucer's **Summoner** repels everyone with his incurable pimply skin disease and garlic breath, and, of course, no one wants to be the object of his attention. Even children flee from him. The Summoner's attempts to overcome his social isolation by playing the clown, wearing odd objects on his head, and pretending to speak Latin are in vain. His only contact with others involves fear and bribery. Fear of false accusation tempts others to offer him bribes, and he, in turn, bribes the real wrong-doers in exchange for not hauling them off to court. "A man's soul is in his purse" is the narrator's comment. Why the narrator does not criticize the Summoner is unclear; perhaps he has seen enough corrupt human behavior to make the Summoner's transgressions noteworthy, or, like everyone else, he does not wish to catch the attention of this harmful man.

Traveling with the Summoner is the **Pardoner**. They are an odd pair: both lonely, both strikingly unattractive, singing a song ironically titled, "Come hither, love, come home!" Contemporary audiences might find reason to feel some compassion for these grotesque men—but the narrator expresses none of the pity he did for the Wife of Bath's deafness. But what redeeming quality does either possess? The Pardoner's bulging eyeballs and waxlike hair, hanging in big hanks down his back until it thins into "rat-tails," are offputting. The narrator notices sexual confusion in the Pardoner. He has no body hair and is compared to a "gelding or a mare," suggesting either impotence, or—like the absurd cake his companion brandishes as a shield—utter uselessness, perhaps even, allegorically, the ultimate impotency of evil.

Understanding the gravity of the Pardoner's transgressions requires some knowledge of the medieval Church's practice of selling relics and pardoning sins. Relics were objects associated with a particular saint and were believed to bear some of the saint's miraculous healing powers. A relic in one's home or congregation was regarded as a blessing, and the Church sanctioned the legitimate sale of these objects. This Pardoner, however, traffics in phony relics, and even boasts about tricking innocent believers into buying a swatch of pillow cloth he touts as having been a piece of Mary's veil. Another corrupt profit-making scheme was selling pardons, or indulgences. Church doctrine held that charitable donations to worthy recipients could earn pardons for the donors' sins. Good deeds done in earnest were believed to shorten a sinner's time in Purgatory and thus hasten arrival in Heaven. Pardoners, as trusted servants of the Church, traveled from congregation to congregation to offer a pardon, receive the donation, and deliver it safely to the beneficiary. Chaucer's shameless Pardoner invents phony beneficiaries and offers illegitimate forgiveness. The donations he pockets for himself. Such transactions constitute mortal as opposed to venial sin because they violate the hierarchy of sacred power that preserves holy the authority of Christendom. Unless he repents (and nothing suggests he will), this particular pardoner is headed for Hell.

Both narrator and host hold distinctive positions on the pilgrimage. **Harry Bailly** is the perfect character to play the role Chaucer has cleverly created in order to make two important additions to his work possible. Only such a gregarious tavern host could plausibly transform a religious pilgrimage into a secular storytelling contest—a diversion from the sacred to the mundane—a temptation the most earnest of people chronically succumb to. By assigning himself the role of organizer and literary critic, Bailly shifts the narrator to the edge of the action, so he can continue his reporting without taking responsibility for what happens along the way. Chaucer scholar Margaret Hallissy calls the inclusion of the Bailly character a "masterstroke." "Harry is a principle of organization, a link holding the tales together and binding them to the pilgrimage frame. . . . [He] provides order [to a] diverse group of pilgrims and tales, keeping them on the right path" (*Companion*, 52). Chaucer's Narrator is the lens through which we get to see the whole spectacle. If he is to succeed in holding our attention, he must be interesting but his skill at observing must be similar to our own: ordinary. E.T. Donaldson argues that Pilgrim Chaucer is . . . merely an average man, or mankind; *homo*, not very *sapiens* to be sure, but with the very best intentions, making his pilgrimage through the world in search of what is good, and showing himself, too frequently, able to recognize the good only when it is spectacularly so. . . . [In] a world consisting mostly of imperfections, accurate evaluations are difficult for a pilgrim who, like mankind, is naïve. . . . [The narrator] belongs to . . . a very old—and very new—tradition of the fallible first person singular.

(Donaldson, *Speaking of Chaucer*, 8)

Summary and Analysis

Introducing his modern English translation of the *Canterbury Tales*, Nevill Coghill writes:

> In all literature there is nothing that touches or resembles the *Prologue*. It is a precise portrait of an entire nation, high and low, old and young, male and female, lay and clerical, learned and ignorant, rogue and righteous, land and sea, town and country, but without extremes. Apart from the stunning clarity, touched with nuance, of the characters presented, the most noticeable thing about them is their normality. They are the perennial progeny of men and women. Sharply individual, together they make a party.
>
> (Coghill, 1951, p. 17)

Before Chaucer sets out, however, he locates this "entire nation [of] high and low" within the farthest reaches of the medieval universe. His own creation begins when the natural world begins—and perennially recommences—its cycle, in April when warm gentle rains loosen the frozen earth to regenerate life. In his celebrated opening sentence of eighteen lines, Chaucer tells us, in essence, that in spring, flowers, birds, and people come to life, and some of those people decide to go on pilgrimages. To this eloquently simple setting, Chaucer adds the mythical world (Zephyrus), the realm of the Zodiac (the Ram), foreign shores, words from Latin and French as well as examples of vernacular English, evocations of springtime from Lucretius, Virgil, and Aeschylus, and, finally, the four elements—earth, air water, fire. The little inn at Southwark and its sundry guests are animated specks in the cosmos.

Chaucer is also speaking metaphorically. No natural drought occurs in March in England, but metaphorical drought comes when winter's harshness reduces human life to the requirements of basic physical survival. When spring eases that struggle, birds become restless with procreative urges, and humans ("pilgrims" according to St. Augustine) are awakened to their need for spiritual regeneration. Chaucer sees yet another difference: birds and humans alike respond to the biological impulses of the springtime, but only humans perceive and follow a source beyond themselves. The Canterbury shrine attracts the pilgrims, or, in Arthur Hoffman's words: "[Nature] impels and supernature draws. 'Go, go, go,' says the bird; 'Come,' says the saint" (Hoffman, Norton, p. 493).

Chaucer has three personas in the *Tales*. Discerning these at the outset makes for more entertaining and instructive reading. Chaucer the public servant is also Chaucer the poet, who, in turn, creates Chaucer the pilgrim/narrator in his own poem. Since Chaucer's audience included friends and colleagues, he was probably circumspect about how he presented himself in his own story. One solution was to create a fictional substitute that both resembled and differed from him. Thus, Chaucer the poet writes those inimitable first lines and,during the pilgrimage, makes witty puns that elude his companions. Chaucer the narrating pilgrim is amiable, eager, a little naïve and undignified, a pilgrim whose tale in the storytelling contest is so "illiterate" (in the host's judgment) that he is ordered to stop telling it. Poet and pilgrim/narrator alike are congenial and tolerant. In E.T. Donaldson's words:

> while the narrator is almost unfailingly simple-minded, the poet who created him and has found a place for his simplicity in the poem—indeed, has sometimes made the meaning depend on it—is anything but simple-minded.
>
> (Donaldson, *Chaucer's Poetry*, p. 878)

Chaucer the poet is omniscient and clairvoyant, and occasionally he "loans" these qualities to his narrator to comment on what he otherwise would be unlikely to know: what the guildsmen's wives, who are not on the pilgrimage, are thinking and what the Reeve's dwelling, which he has never seen, looks like. Generally, the gap between what the poet sees and what the pilgrim describes is large, and Chaucer locates in this space all his wit, complexity, and, above all, his irony.

The plot of the *Tales* is straightforward. The narrator is lodged at the Tabard Inn at Southwark (both actual places, near London), fifty-four miles from the Shrine at Canterbury, a church still and now also a tourist site. He encounters— and quickly joins—twenty-nine pilgrims also preparing for a pilgrimage to pay homage to Saint Thomas of Canterbury for rescuing or protecting them from misfortune. The narrator inquires after each pilgrim and announces his intention to join them. This simple gesture transforms a random grouping into a fellowship. He turns, then, to his audience to inform us about the company he will have for the trip: "What their condition was [their] profession and degree . . . and [their] apparel. . . ." All are portrayed, he cautiously adds, as they appear to him. This qualification effectively absolves him of the responsibility for accuracy and reminds us that appearances are not everything. The result is a set of portraits so lifelike that it is hard not to think of Chaucer as a journalist reporting on a historical event.

But Chaucer was not a journalist but a poet. Despite the high quality of verisimilitude achieved in the work, the pilgrims are fictional creations, stock characters, even, familiar as figures of reverence (the Knight) or hypocrisy (the Pardoner, for one). Chaucer was also writing in the tradition of "estates satire"—a common literary genre in the Middle Ages—that classified people according to their occupation or position in society (their "estate") with an accompanying list of virtues and flaws associated with each category.

One method of creating realistic effect was Chaucer's use of meticulous detail:

The Prioress' table manners and the Miller's wart have their own strongly individualizing effect that pleases us, but if taken merely as picturesque details they lose their significance. People are, indeed, made up of a number of such bits and pieces, but in literature they must be made up into some sort of a whole. That is, reality as we know it consists largely of an infinite number of uncorrelated *minutiae* which the great poet knows how to combine into

36

something we recognize as more real than anything we could ourselves perceive. The Prioress' table manners are far more than a charming accidental detail: actually they convey the very essence of the courteous, misdirected lady. And the Miller's wart helps similarly to make up the sum of what the Miller is: ugly and crude, yet unabashed and vital. These details are not atoms falling in chaos; they are part of Chaucer's cosmos.

(Donaldson, p. 875)

Chaucer also varied the length of each description and focused on the whole body or one individual part. Thomas A. Kirby notes what he calls "the sudden thrust," a quick comment, sounding almost offhand: "one of the most effective [devices] . . . because it gives the impression of being a thought that has just struck the author, who . . . [inserted] it immediately into the description and then . . . resumed a train of thought already begun (*Companion to Chaucer Studies*, 222.) Kirby's favorite example occurs in the Man of Law's portrait, where the narrator quickly deflates the self-importance just ascribed to him ("nowhere there was so busy a man as he") with this satirical remark: "But was less busy than he seemed to be." Satiric commentary on other human failings—usually involving discrepancies between stated and hidden motivations and other gaps in self-knowledge—is achieved by Chaucer's double vision: Pilgrim Chaucer sees; Poet Chaucer sees still more. Chaucer's pilgrims also display plenty of self-revealing behavior as well.

A perennially interesting question in literary studies concerns the attitude of the author toward his characters or creation. Whether speaking in his poet or pilgrim's voice, Chaucer maintains for the most part the disinterested curiosity and amused detachment characteristic of good reporters. Some of the pilgrims are contentious rascals, some are demure and self-effacing, and some, like the Wife of Bath, are, among other things, both charming and outrageous. Is the narrator ever charmed by a character that is not inherently charming? Sometimes his observations are contradictory. Trevor Whittock writes, "[Chaucer's method] is to show an aspect of truth, criticise it, suggest its partiality, set up a counter-truth . . . never quite settle, never give a conclusive answer" (*A Reading of the Canterbury Tales*, Cambridge University Press, 1968, p. 294). There is inconclusiveness in the description of the Franklin. He is a materialistic devotee of epicurean pleasure seeking, but also a follower of Saint Julian, the patron and protector of poor travelers in need of food and shelter. Without the benefit of Freud's insights into the human unconscious or recent discoveries in neurobiology, Chaucer was calmly realistic about human complexity. By contrast, Dante, another famous pilgrim, traveled through Hell, Purgatory, and Paradise. Along the way, he saw and described a host of characters that powerfully affected him: he swooned over the plight of the lovers Paolo and Francesca, disparaged the sullen for their gloomy ingratitude, and angrily condemned a few popes for their hypocrisies and Lucifer for his maniacal self-glorification. But, as D.S. Brewer states:

[Chaucer] never seems angry, and rarely condemns. . . . He maintains a well-bred, courtly, imperturbable front which nothing can shock. In the general *Prologue*, he . . . [has] a connoisseur's appreciation of types. . . . He can enjoy without necessarily liking. He can laugh without feeling affection, accept without approving.

(*Chaucer*, pp. 114–115)

Before embarking Chaucer offers a curious apology that comes in the form of a favor. Do not blame me, he seems to be asking his readers for saying disagreeable things. If crude words are heard, they belong to the pilgrim speaking them, not to Chaucer, poet or pilgrim. Here is his claim to be merely the reporter-in-attendance, which his self-appointed host has made possible.

Having completed the portraits of his companions, Chaucer explains what is to come. Harry Bailly, jovial host of the Tabard Inn, welcomes the pilgrims and proposes a different—and novel—goal for their pilgrimage: not the intended spiritual goal, though he wishes them a good trip to "Blessed" St. Thomas, but a secular prize, a good meal paid for by the others, rewarded to the pilgrim who tells the most entertaining or morally instructive tale on the trip. Why, asks the host, as you are riding along the path, "dumb as stones [with] little pleasure for your bones," not have some fun? Four tales apiece are proposed—two on the way, two on the way back. But again, like life itself, the plan does not unfold as originally proposed. When the *Tales* end, only twenty-two have been told, the pilgrims never arrive at the shrine, and no one gets to eat the promised meal. The host announces his plan to join the pilgrimage, ostensibly to judge their stories, but as likely as not, he joins the group to avoid missing out on the fun he has just proposed.

The Knight's Tale

As the tales begin, the pilgrims join Chaucer by becoming both author and character. The Knight leads off, assuming his proper role as protector of persons and upholder of ideals. The Knight's tale, an elegant chivalric romance set in ancient Athens, touches on all the great universal themes of human existence. Love, conflict, and loss dominate this tale; death begins and ends it. Theseus, duke of Athens, returning from conquering the Amazons accompanied by his new bride Queen Hippolita and her sister Emily, is confronted by a group of women in black mourning dress. Grasping onto his horse's bridle, the women tell their terrible story of how Creon, the new ruler of Thebes following Oedipus, has denied burial to their slain husbands and brothers. Theseus takes pity on them and changes his course. Instead of returning home to celebrate victory, he rides off with traditional knightly valor (which the knight enjoys mentioning) to right the wrongs these women have suffered. In the ensuing battle, Creon is killed and two knights, united by blood—Arcite and Palamon—are found alive in a pile of dead bodies. Theseus could have ordered them killed but—mercy being part of the divine order—condemns them instead to life imprisonment in a tower in Athens, where, one spring morning, they notice from the window the pure and beautiful Emily walking in the garden. In an instant they are love struck, and their kinship is replaced by a passionate rivalry.

Here we are introduced to the concept of "courtly love," a literary, and some think, purely legendary, tradition of a highly specialized love that originated in southern France in the twelfth century. Famous instances of courtly love include those of Tristan for Iseult and Sir Lancelot for Queen Guinevere. Features of courtly love include suddenly falling in love (both knights are forever transfigured by one eye-piercing glance at Emily) and the impossibility of ever consummating the love (the knights are locked away forever in a tower, and Emily is blithely oblivious to the men and the storm of passion she has churned up). Palamon and Arcite endure the longings and agonies of courtly love even after each gets out of the tower. Courtly love was revered as an emotion that only the heart of a noble man could experience. Chaucer does not use the term, but he would have been well-acquainted with the tradition. *Tales* translator Nevill Coghill points out that the love between husband and wife in Chaucer's time was not assumed to have such an impossibly passionate element. That was preserved for the courtly lover whose typical situation

> was to be plunged in a secret ... illicit ... passion for some seemingly unattainable and pedestalized lady. Before his mistress a lover was prostrate, wounded to death by her beauty, killed by her disdain. ... A smile from her was ... a gracious reward for twenty years of painful adoration. All Chaucer's heroes regard love when it comes upon them as the most beautiful of absolute disasters, an agony as much desired as bemoaned, ever to be pursued, never to be betrayed.
>
> (Introduction, Penguin translation
> of *The Canterbury Tales*, p. 12)

Through an influential friend, Arcite is released from the tower but is banished forever from his homeland. He returns, however, in disguise, and one day confronts Palamon who has escaped from the tower and is wandering in the woods, lovesick for Emily. Still rivals, the knights agree to duel for Emily's love the next day. Theseus comes across the duelers, intervenes, discovers their identities, considers again authorizing their deaths and is prevailed upon again by women requesting mercy. Theseus points out that Emily remains unaware of her role in this drama (one of the few comic details in this otherwise high-minded tale), then devotes himself to organizing an elaborate tournament to take place in a year that will decide the fate of all three.

At this point in the Knight's tale, we can begin to discern the multiple dualities underpinning and animating the story: love and warfare, man and woman, age and youth, Thebes and Athens, Theseus and Creon, Palamon and Arcite, judgment and mercy, harmony and chaos, loyalty and rivalry, freedom and imprisonment, Venus and Mars. These dualities reflect the ancient (pre-Christian) view that order in the world came about through the tension and balance of opposing forces. Chaos always threatened, and its myriad manifestations were influenced by the gods and personified in the figure of Fortuna with her Wheel of Fortune. Fortuna stood for all the capricious forces in the universe—operating beyond the reach of human understanding— that could, with a turn of the wheel, bring about a sudden reversal of fortune in the life of an individual or a nation.

The Knight's tale has many examples of Chance interrupting the plans humans have set for themselves by creating "coincidences" that change the course of a life. Theseus's plan for his victorious return is disrupted by the wailing women; two blood-related knights are the sole survivors of a massacre; an unanticipated act of mercy spares the knights' lives; the two then fall in love with the same woman. These coincidences could be the contrivances of narrative, but they are not unbelievable. The pivotal events that follow become increasingly unlikely, even preposterous. Both Palamon and Arcite escape separately from the tower but end up in the same woods at the same time; Theseus comes upon them as they are dueling just in time to intercede and prevent additional tragedy; mercy intervenes to save them again; and, at the end, Arcite makes his dramatic and unanticipated fall from victory to death. Though unlikely to the point of absurdity, these events were understood to be expressions of divine will.

The gods, in fact, are a visual part of the grand display. Theseus constructs a trio of shrines honoring Venus, Diana, and Mars. Palamon, allied with Venus, goes secretly to her shrine the night before the contest to pray for Emily's love and asks to be slain if he fails. Emily goes to Diana's shrine hoping to have her declaration of female independence blessed. Diana, however, tells Emily she must marry the victorious knight. Arcite, allied with Mars, visits his shrine to pray for victory the next day and hears the word "Victory."

Theseus has decreed that no lethal weapons be used. The winner is he whose side has—of the hundred men fighting with each knight—the highest number still standing at the end of the tournament. After fierce battling, Palamon is wounded and Arcite declared the victor by Theseus. Then a most unlikely thing happens. Up in the heavens, according to the knight's rendition of this ancient story, there is dissension about the results, and Saturn, god of mishap, arranges to have a force akin to a thunderbolt strike the earth near the spot where Arcite is proudly astride his horse. The startled animal bolts, and Arcite falls to the ground, gravely wounded. A detailed account is given of the medieval medical strategies used to restore Arcite to health, but these fail. For a few fleeting moments, Arcite is atop Fortuna's Wheel, but, as ancient traditions taught, the moment is precarious and not to be trusted. Beyond the sight and understanding of all assembled, Chance has intervened. In an instant the fates of Emily and the knights have been inexplicably redirected.

In the interval between the wounding and death of Arcite, Theseus emerges as the figure of order and restoration. A true leader, he comforts and converses with Arcite, whose imminent death raises for all the profound and perennial questions of how justice is determined, why the innocent suffer, and the ultimate question: "What is this world? What does man ask to have?" Before he dies, Arcite calls Palamon and Emily to his bedside. A loving and noble reconciliation ensues. The Knight holds the Christian belief in an afterlife (as the pagan characters in his story do not), but he seems bewildered as he describes the moment of Arcite's death. He tells the pilgrims:

"[Arcite's] spirit changed its house and went away / Where I came never—where I cannot say, / And so am silent. I am no divine." Everyone weeps in loud lamentation for the death of the young knight, who receives the traditional pagan rite of cremation. In this sober first tale of the pilgrimage, there are few comic moments, but the knight unintentionally provides some when he insists he has not enough time to tell about all the preparations made for Arcite's sepulcher and then at length does just that.

After years of mourning, Theseus summons Palamon and Emily separately and announces to the assembled citizens that he will now permit their marriage: "So, ere we make departure from this place, / I rule that of two sorrows we endeavor / To make one perfect joy, to last forever." In the great formal speech that precedes this announcement, however, Theseus acknowledged that life's mutability is its only certain feature. There is no contradiction here. Theseus has stated what it is that humans can attempt to do, not what they can control. It is the "First Great Cause and Mover of all above" that "with high intent" made the world. Because this "[Mover] well knew why He did, and what He meant," humans must take comfort knowing that every mysterious and apparently merciless event and outcome are part of the supreme order. Wisdom, he memorably concludes, is "[to] make a virtue of necessity. . . ." So he proposes what he can do: restore order by creating one joy out of two sorrows. The Knight offers similar wisdom: "It is a good thing for a man to bear himself with equanimity / for one is constantly keeping appointments one never made."

The Knight's tale is the longest and the most metaphysical in content—appropriate for a first tale because it provides a framework for all the stories that follow. Its moral instruction includes the recognition that passionate love like that afflicting Palamon and Arcite can imprison the spirit more effectively than the walls of the tower. Indeed, all of human life is itself a prison: we cannot make things happen as we wish nor are we in charge of our own fate. Theseus's father had to remind his son that "[this] world is but a thoroughfare of woe / And we are pilgrims passing to and fro. . . ." One purpose of Christian pilgrimage is achieving awareness of these worldly constraints and attempting to throw them off in preparation for the afterlife. The Knight's tale reminds the pilgrims of a lesson they have already learned.

The Miller's Tale

The host shares the general enthusiasm for the Knight's tale and is eager to get on with the contest. He looks to the Monk for the next tale, but so much for order and planning: the drunken Miller, with his bulky frame, insists vociferously on being next. The Host seems to have no choice besides getting out of the way. These passages linking the tales are occasions for additional character development and observation of social interactions. For example, the Miller's jarring interruption is superficially inappropriate (and rude), but it is also entirely plausible. Chaucer scholar George Lyman Kittredge writes:

> Travel, as everybody knows, is for the time being a mighty leveller of social distinctions, particularly when its concomitants throw the voyagers together while at the same time isolating them from the rest of the world. . . . The occasion [of a pilgrimage] . . . was both religious and social; and the various Pilgrims, knowing that all men are equal in God's sight, were not indisposed to sink their differences of rank for nonce [occasion]. . . .
>
> (Kittredge, *Chaucer and His Poetry*, pp. 158–160)

Just as the Miller begins, the Reeve makes his own interruption—an indignant protest against drunkenness and the possibility that the Miller's story will cast unfair aspersions on wives. The Miller suggest subtly that the Reeve's worries are more about himself, then adds this bit of advice: "One shouldn't be too inquisitive in life / Either about God's secrets or one's wife." The narrator advises the audience to turn the page or the ear away from the ensuing tale, namely a "churl's tale" marked by vulgarity or indecorous actions described in bawdy language. It is unlikely, however, this warning is heeded by anyone in attendance.

John C. Hirsh calls the *Miller's Tale* a "riotous reprise of the *Knight's Tale*" (p. 136). In amusing contrast to the stately Knight's elegance is the Miller's maladroit appearance (is he on or off his horse?) and crude "huffing and swearing" about his own "noble legend." The story the Miller tells is also ancient, but Chaucer's additional details and irony make it the greatest comic poem in English.

Two young men—Nicholas the Oxford student who rents a room in the home of old John the carpenter, and Absalom the curly-headed parish clerk who worries about having bad breath—are lusting after the same woman, Alison, John's young wife. (In medieval times, people looked with ridicule at old men taking young girls to wife.) Alison, no Emily-like model of pristine femininity, is as lecherous as the men who pursue her. Stuck with a geezer for a husband, she is happy to cavort with Nicholas.

With his "educated" wit, Nicholas invents a strategy to steal a few secret hours with Alison. Citing mysterious warnings emanating from the position of the moon and stars, Nicholas persuades John that a second flood of biblical proportions is on its way to drown the world "next Monday a quarter way through night." John reacts with predictable fearfulness for his own and his "dear wife's" life and agrees to the fantastic remedy Nicholas proposes to save all three of them. On the fated night, each will gather enough food for a one-day flood and sleep separately in a large, heavy-duty kneading tub, attached to the ceiling and strategically arranged to allow the young lovers to escape to the first floor bedroom, out of John's hearing. Inspired by Nicholas's image of their Noahlike escape from the flood, John consents to the plan.

But one trick is not enough for this boisterous tale. While Nicholas and Alison are off in the bedroom, Absalom, who has not given up hope of winning Alison's favor and has gone to the absurd length of playing the part of Herod in the village play to get her attention, now arrives eagerly at her window. Absalom's efforts have not gone well ("However Absalom might blow his horn / His labour won him nothing but her scorn / She looked upon him as her private ape / And held his wooing all a jape."), but he remains optimistic. Alison agrees to a kiss if he will then go away, but when he leans through the window, he gets not Alison's lovely face but her bottom and something other than a kiss. Over the centuries, readers have had a fine time with this scene. "It is a moment of awful comedy" is Derek Brewer's understated summary.

The second trick engenders a third, as cruel as it is funny. Enraged, the deflated Absalom seeks revenge by returning to the same window that same night intending to reward a second kiss with a red-hot sharpened ploughshare. Hearing Absalom again serenading Alison, Nicholas decides to get into the act with a trick of his own and sticks his own rear out the window. When Nicholas screams "Water!", John thinks the flood is coming and cuts the ropes. He and his "rescue boat" crash to the floor, injuring but not killing him. The ensuing commotion brings all the villagers rushing to see what is the matter. Everyone gathers around laughing heartily at the spectacle.

Brewer writes:

> The wife is the center of . . . attention, but the story is not about her: it is not even primarily about the men who circle around her as a sexual object: the story is, at its deepest or, as we may well say, at its lowest level, the articulation of a deliberately fantastic insult, common to all languages of Europe . . . in the Middle Ages[:] "Kiss my arse." . . . Furthermore, the repetition of the first kiss by the burning second one produces further parody— we have all heard of burning kisses. . . .We may well remember Aristotle's remark that comedy portrays people as worse than they usually are. Let us hope it is true. In origin the story is anti-feminist. . . . The implication is that women trick men and make them suffer. But comedy is always ambivalent. And it takes two to play the wife's game. . . . Chaucer is very sympathetic to women and he makes the wife very charming and attractive, though he mocks her too.

(Brewer, *A New Introduction to Chaucer*, pp. 283–284)

An interesting contrast to the Knight's tale about the necessity for stoic acceptance of life is the Miller's jolly approval of practical jokes as a legitimate—if quite parochial—way to live.

The Reeve's Tale

Once a carpenter himself, Oswald the Reeve is unhappy with the Miller's tale because it makes fun of old John. So he turns around and tells a tale that makes fun of a miller. (Both tales remind us that disharmony between "townies" and students is centuries old.) Symkin, a miller, lives with his wife, their eligible but not beautiful daughter, and an infant. From this simple-looking tale, we learn something complex about medieval life. The Miller's wife is of nobler birth than her husband. A pretentious man, he insisted on marrying a woman of higher class because with her he could strut around feeling superior to others of his class. He acquired his wife because, as it happened, she was noble, but not entirely, "being the daughter of a celibate priest." This celibate father provided her with education and a dowry, then married her off to the miller because no one of the nobler classes would take her as a wife.

The miller cheats his customers by adding his thumb to the weighing machine before grinding. Two students who have brought their university's store of grain for milling know about his tricks and plan to outsmart him. Feigning interest in the milling process, each student stands at the beginning and end point to ensure that no grain gets siphoned off to the miller. But the miller outsmarts the students by untying their horse when they are not looking and stealing a half bushel of the measured grain while they are off chasing the escaped animal. This is a reversal the students cannot let stand. They ask to spend the night in the miller's snug house. During the night, they manage to seduce the miller's wife and daughter, cuckolding the miller. In the darkness of predawn, one student tries to sneak back into the bed he had been sharing with the other student to brag about his nocturnal exploits. But he get in the wrong bed, and it is the miller who hears how his guest has had sex with his daughter "three times in this short night."

The students have more than evened the score. With his final image of a deflated and cuckolded miller sprawled and bleeding on the floor, the Reeve has made his point, too.

The Miller's and Reeve's tales are examples of a medieval literary genre known as *fabliau*. Originating in twelfth-century France, fabliaux are short comic stories in verse about low- or middle-class people engaged in improbable and obscene antics. Fabliaux generally present a sordid, although sometimes playful, picture of life. Margaret Hallissey points out that "both [tales] are not only actually shorter but move at a much faster pace than did the 'Knight's Tale.' The slow, stately pace of the romance lends dignity and high seriousness. In contrast, the *fabliau* plot moves along rapidly, as befits a joke" (Hallissey, 88).

The Reeve's tale is also known as a churl's tale, as are those of the Miller, Merchant, and Friar. Winthrop Wetherbee, discussing the division in medieval society between the "gentles" and the "churls," calls the Miller "the most genial of the churls" but of the others he writes:

> Their viewpoint is materialistic and amoral but, with no regard for orthodox social and religious values, they exhibit a strong, unwieldy aptitude for social criticism. Nearly all their tales are comic, but their lives and the lives of their characters are often so distorted by ambition, the commercializing of social relations, or the bitterness of old age as to make it impossible for them to pursue even the elemental goods of food, drink, and sex in a straightforward way.
>
> (Wetherbee, 56)

The Cook's Tale

The Cook takes his turn to chide the Host and warns that he will tell a host tale soon. For now he tells about Peterkin, a lazy and unruly apprentice whose tolerant master finally throws him out. Peterkin takes up with a thief whose wife "went whoring for a living." This tale was probably going to develop further, but Chaucer left it unfinished.

The Man of Law's Tale

The host may think there has been enough laughing and ribaldry, so he calls on the lawyer, perhaps expecting a more substantial tale. After claiming not to remember any "pithy" stories that Chaucer has not already himself told, the lawyer launches into a long somber tale about Constance, a young woman living happily with her parents (her father is the emperor of Rome). Constance's unusual beauty, humility, faith, and innocence—the ideal of medieval femininity—attracts the attention of a faraway sultan who has her brought on reputation alone to his kingdom to be his wife. True to the ideal, Constance does not protest and with great sorrow resigns herself to a new life with an unknown man. This unhappiness is the first in an improbably long string of misadventures that she must undergo. Her mother-in-law expresses resentment over her son's conversion from Islam to Christianity, by having him and all the Christians in Constance's retinue chopped into pieces during a celebratory feast. Only Constance is spared, the lawyer suggests, because God has rescued his faithful servant. But more punishment awaits her: she is set adrift in a rudderless boat and left to flounder on the high seas. Many readers view Constance's unmitigated suffering allegorically as the plight all human beings must endure in this unfathomable and ever-perilous universe. She survives a shipwreck, is rescued and kindly treated for a brief period, but then again abandoned to greater hardship. When she and the kind king she marries have a child, another hateful mother (the king's) intervenes maliciously to inform her son away on some battlefield that his infant is a "fiend"—a grotesquely disfigured creature signifying punishment for some great sin. Despite the king's message averring his love for both wife and child, his mother orders Constance set adrift at sea again. This somber tale raises the darkest questions for believers: why does a loving God permit evil to fall upon the innocent and faithful like Constance? Like the Old Testament figure Job who God tested with a series of afflictions, Constance remains steadfast in her faithfulness to God and is ultimately rescued and reunited with her husband and her parents. Instruction—not entertainment—is the purpose of this tale: those of patient faith will not ultimately be abandoned by God.

The Shipman's Tale

Money and its power to undermine, even substitute for, human relationships is the theme of the Shipman's tale. The nameless (generic) merchant is thought to be wise because he is rich—a theory that will be upended by the tale. An attentive reader will note that the speaker of the tale turns briefly at the beginning from male to female: from "he had a wife . . . [a] thing which causes more pecunial dearth" to "the silly husband always has to pay . . . to array our bodies to enhance his reputation. . . ." Nothing is gained by this confusion, and it can be assumed to be one of the unfinished aspects of the *Tales*.

Neither gender looks virtuous in this tale, but the male speaker who debases a wife by referring to her as a "thing" is especially offensive. Medieval misogyny is reflected by other assumptions in the tale, a prominent one being that vanity causes women to procure money from someone, if not the husband, then a lover. Such triangulation has the power to profoundly disrupt an orderly society, but not in this tale. The Shipman's narration exposes how money circulates when and wherever it is needed, especially for narcissistic and sexual indulgence. Love, loyalty, beauty, and relationships are commodities, not ideals in this tale. Interestingly, this impoverished way of life does not appear to seriously harm anyone. The tale, neither particularly instructive nor entertaining, discusses individuals so disfigured by vanity they cannot notice what they are missing.

The Prioress's Tale

The Prioress begins her tale praising the Lord for all his majesty and Mary for the complex miracle she embodies. We remember from the *Prologue* that she possesses an extravagant sympathy for dogs and trapped mice but none for her fellow humans, a serious failing for a nun. Here, by contrast, her story is about an exceptionally pure child who is drawn to a sacred song whose words in Latin he cannot understand.

An older student teaches him the words, which the boy feels compelled to learn by heart and does so at the expense of his schoolwork. The story suddenly turns grim when the boy is killed on his way to school and thrown into a ditch by the Jews in the neighborhood who are said to have been offended by his singing.

Anti-Semitism existed in the Middle Ages, but the Catholic Church at the time condemned it, and Chaucer himself was not associated with it. The Prioress's intense but distorted sympathies have made for an intense but distorted religious faith. Jesus directs the frantic mother to the boy's body and, at the moment of discovery, this "little jewel of martyrdom" begins to sing his memorized song for all to hear. The guilty Jews are meted out an Old Testament–style justice—"Evils shall meet the evils they deserve." They are killed by "[being] drawn apart by horses . . . then hanged from a cart." Before his burial the little boy sings again and tells the astonished mourners that the miracle his life has become is the work of the Virgin Mother Mary. The boy's mother, however, cannot be reconciled. She joins the circle of bereaved women in the Bible who have lost a child.

The Tale of Sir Topaz

The Pilgrims are subdued by this tale of martyrdom and miracle, but the host—after a reverent interval—addresses the narrator, mentions his plump and elfish form, and demands a "tale of mirth." The narrator feigns stupidity and warns everyone not to expect much. Chaucer must have been much amused with this playfully satirical tale he invents for his alter ego to tell. Before he begins, he allows himself to be compared to a doll (a "poppet") in a woman's embrace—hardly a flattering image. His tale turns out to be about an unchivalrous knight, skilled at archery and wrestling, but not at exhibiting bravery before an enemy or even at getting on his horse.

Understanding Chaucer's tale requires knowledge of the courtly romance (discussed in the Knight's tale) of which this is a parody. Seeking an adventure that will confirm his bravery and prowess, this not particularly handsome fellow, all red and white in the face, mounts ("clambers on") his horse with difficulty and rides through the intoxicating springtime woods encountering "monsters" in the form of rabbits and deer. We are told that the knight wearied of galloping across the grass, but it is his poor out-of-shape sweating horse that is making all the effort. In a swoon on the grass, Topaz has a knightlike dream of his lady love, a fantastical Elf Queen. He doesn't meet up with her, though. Instead, he comes across a menacing giant named Sir Elephant who challenges him to a duel—just the adventure he desires. Unwilling to fight without his armor, Sir Topaz flings a few warning insults at the giant as he rushes off. Back home he suits himself up inside three layers of armor and rallies his kinsmen for support as he charges off to conquer his adversary, who has become more frightful in the interim by acquiring two more heads.

E.T. Donaldson calls this tale one of Chaucer's best jokes. He observes that there is satire in style as well as content. The appropriate meter for these romances was a steady dogtrot rhythm suggestive of confident determination, but the meter conveying Sir Topaz on his adventure "marches martially on through thick and thin with the sense of great deeds being done while Sir [Topaz] himself is sometimes moving backwards, sometimes listening to romances of popes and cardinals, sometimes merely lying down on the soft grass to dream about an elf-queen" (Donaldson, *Chaucer's Poetry*, p. 936).

The poet's fun is not over yet. He watches himself being humiliated by the indignant host who demands that he halt his "dreary rhyming [that's] not worth a turd!" The narrator apologizes and offers up a new tale.

The Tale of Melibee

Instead of the doggerel verse that has so offended the host, Chaucer presents a prose tale that is more of a lengthy sermon, more tedious than harsh. It concerns an offense done to Melibee's wife, Dame Prudence, and daughter, Sophia (Wisdom), by figures representing the trio of evils—world, flesh, and the devil. A debate ensues about what is the proper punishment to mete out to the captured wrong-doers. Ethical authorities are cited from the Old and New Testaments, classical sages such as Seneca and Cicero, Saint Gregory and Pope Innocent. "Women are wicked" is Melibee's first argument, but his wife (who represents prudence but not passion) emerges as the persuasive figure. After one thousand lines, nothing is heard of Sophia's fate, but prudence and forgiveness have been established as superior to personal revenge and warfare as instruments of social and personal governance.

The Monk's Tale

The host's reaction to Melibee's tale is Chaucer's chance to reveal his character as something other than jolly. At home, he reports, he feels harassed by a wife who vociferously urges revenge at the slightest slight. He laments that she is not more like Dame Prudence. Then he calls on the Monk for the next story, noting in passing the latter's somewhat robust appearance not commonly befitting a monk. The Monk's tale is a recounting of great figures who have fallen from grace or positions of authority, beginning with Lucifer on through Julius Caesar and Croesus. Each story illustrates the medieval (not classical) notion of tragedy: joy and prosperity inevitably give way to misery and failure. The Monk is prepared to give more examples of this phenomenon—he claims to have one hundred in his memory—but is stopped when the Knight, suddenly assuming authority, expresses concern that the Pilgrims (and he) are bored by these sad tales. He chides the Monk for not following the rules about making the trip pleasant for all. The Knight wants to hear "gladsome" stories about folks on the opposite trajectory.

The Nun's Priest Tale

We know nothing of the nun's priest except his name, Sir John, and the unexceptional goodness of his nature. He offers a retelling of an Aesop fable, set in a poor widow's busy barnyard. The tale recounts a spirited argument between two chickens—Chanticleer, the splendid red, gold, and black rooster famous for his superlative crowing, and his "damsel" Pertelote, his favorite of seven hens and his true love, who returns his affections. One night a dreadful dream portending his demise startles Chanticleer out of his sleep on the perch. His frightful screams awaken Pertelote, nestled against him. Pertelote is not impressed by dreams and scorns her mate's fearfulness as shameful and cowardly. His royal image now deflated in her eyes, Pertelote announces that she is no longer in love with him. To this injury, she adds one biting insult—she calls him a "timorous poltroon!"—and one humiliating piece of advice: "To purge your cowardly vapors, take a laxative!"

Impervious to insult, Chanticleer gives an impressive list of historical incidents reliably proving that dire consequences do indeed come from ignoring prophetic dreams. Victims of this error of judgment form an illustrious group (Hector falling to Achilles is one), which Chanticleer imagines himself about to join. He denounces again Pertelote's foul remedies and praises the "scarlet loveliness about [her] eyes." Having regained his cocksure composure, he addresses her in Latin. "Mulier est hominus confusion . . ." he says, translating (incompletely), "Woman is man's delight and all his bliss."

In the flourish of love's pride, Chanticleer forgets his own warning and unwisely hops off the perch onto the barnyard to come face to face with the fabled red and yellow fox. Exhibiting his renowned cleverness, the fox feigns flattery and challenges the famous rooster to show off his talent. Chanticleer allows "flattery to ravish reason," and, as he stretches high to crow, is grabbed ignominiously by the fox and hauled away. As the fox waits in the cabbage patch, the tone of the fable becomes unmistakably mock heroic: the fox is a "new Iscariot," Pertelote is as guilty as Eve in the Garden, and the hens screeching in despair are likened to the wailing women of Troy. At this point the Nun's Priest attempts to address the great issues raised in the commotion. What brought Chanticleer to his demise? Was he "incapable of smelling treason"? Did pride precede his fall? Was Pertelote, like all women, once again to blame? Did God foresee this event, and, if so, could it have been prevented? The Priest is not up to solving this "vexing matter of predestination," but raising it gives substance to this otherwise entertaining story.

We expect Chanticleer to die, but he does not. Fortuna's whimsy affects chickens too. Chanticleer outfoxes the fox by persuading him to let go just a minute to warn off the converging rescue party of squawking hens, swarming bees, a bellowing cow and calf, squealing pigs, Molly the sheep, the old widow and her dogs, Coll, Talbot, Bran, and Shaggy. The fox cannot resist a chance to turn around and call them all a bunch of "saucy bumpkins," so he opens his mouth and Chanticleer escapes. The fox is left with only his own ranting, and all listeners are reminded of the tale's great lesson on resisting flattery.

In some manuscripts, an epilogue follows in which the host seems to suggest that the Priest might have wished for a "few hens to trod on" himself.

The Wife of Bath's Tale

The Wife of Bath seems to have violated every rule of decorum for widows in her robust defiance of tradition: no somber expression, no plain attire but boisterous color and irrepressible personality. Alison (we later learn her name) believes, or rather asserts, that experience, not tradition, is authority enough for her and lets it be known that she has used her experience with five husbands (a sixth is anticipated) to examine Christian teachings on marriage.

Of the five husbands, three were old, rich, and decent, and she laughs recalling how hard she had to work to keep her aging spouses sexually active and functioning to her satisfaction. Her fourth husband was a "reveler" with a "paramour," whom, for revenge, she tormented with audacious flirting of her own, including with the man who becomes her fifth and favorite husband. The Wife's best-known trait appears most delightfully in the scene depicting the fourth's funeral service. The newly widowed woman hides her absence of grief behind a veil, and falls into a lusty swoon at the sight of her next husband's legs as he stands behind the coffin. Twenty years separate these two in age, but Alison is fully his match because, as she boldly reports, the influences of Venus and Mars converging at her birth gave her an insuppressible sexual appetite.

But the fourth, as it turns out, is the reason she is deaf. A month into the marriage, with all her treasure now under his control, he turns into a woman-hating scold who interminably cites examples from history of woman's wickedness. "Better," he says, "to share your habitation with lion, dragon, or abomination than with a woman given to reproof." Maddened, she tears three pages from his book, and he, in turn, strikes her on the head hard enough to cause deafness. Reconciliation comes on her terms: she recovers all her treasure and assumes full responsibility for her life.

Although the Wife of Bath is rendered with wonderful comic and individualizing detail, she belongs to an anti-feminist tradition of powerful women who are accused of undermining men and making their lives miserable. By Chaucer's time, according to E.T. Donaldson, the notion of a woman as a kind of monster was widely held and respected despite men's own actual experiences to the contrary.

> The Wife of Bath's mission . . . is to summarize in her own personality everything that has been said against women for hundreds of years. . . . One supposes that when he first thought of her Chaucer [had the] mischievous idea of forcing the reader to compare the Wife, representing woman in her traditionally lecherous . . . avaricious . . . domineering . . . pragmatic form, with women as the reader knew them: the Wife would be placed before her . . . perpetuators and . . . allowed to say, "You made me what I am today: I hope you're satisfied." Such a plan shows the characteristic double-edge of Chaucerian satire: the creators of the tradition, and contemporary men who professed to believe it, are satirized because the character is a monstrous perversion of what experience shows; but women are satirized too, because in many of her characteristics, interwoven with the monstrosities, the Wife of Bath is precisely what experience teaches. Chaucer was able here—as so often elsewhere—to have it both ways.
>
> (Donaldson, p. 914)

He goes on to say that better than the "superbly realized" distortion of womanhood achieved by Chaucer in her portrayal is his successful weaving of all her traits into a complex and commendably human character. All her tendencies can be seen as

> the significant probings of an individual trying to live happily in a world governed by rules that even the most aware of women can only imperfectly understand. If the Wife of Bath has not wholly won the game, she has by no means capitulated. There remains for her the fun she had in handling her men . . . the fun she has had in life itself. . . . The Wife [at the end of her Prologue] ceases to be a very funny parody of a woman invented by women-haters . . . or in a way a woman fascinating for her intense individuality . . . [or even] a woman at all, and becomes instead a high and gallant symbol of a humanity in which weakness and fortitude are inextricably mingled. [When] she surveys her youth with both regret and blessing for what has passed she seems to enlarge the boundaries of human consciousness, so that mankind itself becomes more vital because of her. (915)

It is clear that Donaldson, writing so persuasively in the 1950s, did so without benefit of the knowledge about these rules that "aware women" in recent decades have devoted their scholarly lives to achieving. Many have written on the Wife of Bath with valuable new perspectives, but Donaldson celebrates the prominence she continues to hold in our imaginations.

Before the Wife begins her tale, the Friar and the Summoner have a spat, which the host interrupts because he is so eager to hear what she has to tell. The idea she has been promoting all along is her wish to control her own life. It makes sense that in her tale, set in King Arthur's mythical kingdom, she turns people and the world toward her vision. The tale begins when a "lusty" bachelor knight rapes a maiden and is condemned to lose his head. Once again, women successfully intervene to save a life. This time, with the king's permission, they are authorized to decide the knight's fate. They charge the knight on pain of death with taking a year and a day to find the answer to the question: What do women most desire?

Somewhat sullenly the spared knight sets off and, despite asking everyone at every door, finds "no two people willing to agree." "Honor," "gorgeous clothes," "fun in bed," and "flattery" are common responses, but a few say "freedom to do exactly what we please." Despairing of getting the right answer, the knight heads back on the last day of his quest. On the path he encounters twenty-four ladies dancing who vanish inconveniently, leaving only a foul-looking hag who offers him the wisdom of old age. In exchange for a promise to do the next thing she asks of him, the woman "croons her gospel [into] his ear": women want sovereignty over husband, lover, and their own lives. When the knight announces the answer, "not one [woman] shook her head [in contradiction]." "He's saved his life!" they all acclaim. The old woman steps up to claim her wish, which is that the knight marry her, and the women of the court make him keep his promise. The knight does not react graciously. Calling it a "foul alliance," he grumpily consents to the union showing not a speck of gratitude for the sparing of his life. On his wedding night he "twists and wallows desperately," full of revulsion for his new wife's ugliness, old age, and low birth. The wise and magnanimous old woman cleverly tricks him into experiencing the loss of control that he has inflicted on the maiden. Then she sets to proving that all his objections to her are superficial, based on arrogance and "hardly worth a hen." The knight learns from her teaching and surrenders to her sovereignty. He is rewarded for his endurance and new insight by the sudden transformation of the old woman into a beautiful maiden and given the assurance that marital harmony will result from a more balanced union between men and women.

This lesson about the power of experience to transform people and of transformation to create new and better life is worthy of the Wife of Bath. She uses her last words to ask God to "send a pestilence" to men everywhere who have not yet learned the lesson she has imparted.

The Friar's Tale

After trading insults with the Summoner, the Friar tells about an especially corrupt one who meets up with a yeoman who later identifies himself as a "fiend from Hell." This revelation seems not to alarm the Summoner. Since both are pursuing as big a "take" for themselves as they can find, they form a "brotherly" pact "for eternity" to aid each other's efforts. Unlike the Summoner, the fiend has one standard for their deceptive practice: the offending person must mean what he or she says or does. The Summoner falsely accuses a poor woman and then offers a bribe for not turning her in. The woman responds with a curse, and the fiend summarily dispatches the Summoner to Hell.

The Summoner's Tale

The Summoner cannot begin his tale until he vents his rage at the Friar's mendacity. Friars, he rants, end up in Hell under Lucifer's tail, in a nest in his "arse." This lively utterance calms him sufficiently to begin his narration, but his rage against friars creeps back in. He tells of a friar who sells "trentles" (masses for the dead) but erases the donor's name without providing the promised prayers. The host intervenes to tell the disruptive Friar to "Shut up!" The friar of the tale resumes his corrupt ways when he visits Thomas, a rich, bedridden acquaintance, not fooled by his false promises. Thomas calls the friar to his bedside promising that treasure is hidden beneath his buttocks. When the friar dives in for the prize he is met with an expulsion of gas, which Thomas instructs him to share with his cohorts. This is the second instance in the *Tales* of an especially offensive gift. Like the Millers Tale, the Summoner's story is a *fabliau*, and with its humiliating outcome forms a complementary grouping with the Friar's Tale. The Reeve who is himself a scoundrel calls these two cheats "beguilers beguiled."

The Clerk's Tale

The host rouses the Oxford student out of his "abstruse meditation" and asks for a "lively" tale in plain speech, neither boring nor depressing. (He knows what he wants!) The tale, belonging to Chaucer's group of marriage tales, describes Walter, ruler of fertile lands in Italy, being approached by concerned citizens to urge him to marry and produce an heir. With implausible indifference he consents and a marriage feast is prepared. On the marriage day, Walter, in royal flourish, descends on a peasant village cottage and announces to the lovely and hardworking Griselda that she is his choice. Quaking at his presence and the terms he insists on—"When I say 'Yes' you never shall say 'No'—she does not know how to refuse the offer and so consents.

Early in the marriage Walter becomes obsessed with testing Griselda's constancy, and, without provocation, inflicts on her a series of cruel experiments, beginning with taking her firstborn, a daughter, and pretending to have it killed. Griselda's silent acquiescence is not enough proof so he takes away the second child, a boy. Griselda's unspeakable grief is expressed in her silence, but she remains devoted. Walter continues to exercise his cruel will and some readers speculate that Chaucer is constructing an allegory here using Griselda, like Constance before her, to represent all souls faithfully enduring God's mysterious ways. But, as Helen Philllips points out:

> "Walter's bullying of Griselda is not, like God's, a 'governaunce' . . . designed for the recipient's good . . . or to exercise our moral strength or teach us constancy: Chaucer has shown it as illogical, purposeless, unjustifiable and born out of some human weakness in the human husband. . . . [The tale] is a bizarre plot, offensive to morality and sensitivity, whether medieval or modern. (Phillips, pp. 116–117)

The still-alive children are restored to Griselda, but Chaucer with his known sympathy for women steps in at the end to admonish husbands not to test their wives' patience and urge wives to "stand up . . . [and] prevail!"

The Merchant's Tale

Married for two months, the Merchant explodes with anger at the Clerk's portrait of a long-suffering wife. His own wife he calls "the worst there could be" and begins a tale that will give lengthy consideration to the joys and challenges of marriage but, in the end, will reflect his own bitterness.

His tale concerns a lustful rich Knight named January, who late in age gets a "violent" urge to marry and chooses for a wife Fresh May, less classy than he, but much younger and ravishing. Although January fancies himself "coltish," May finds his sexual prowess to be "not worth a bean," and develops instead a passion for her husband's young squire, Damian.

References to the Garden of Eden are unmistakable. January constructs a luxuriant garden for private marital pleasure, but one summer day there he suddenly becomes blind. Now fearfully jealous, he keeps May within reach at all times, thus preventing her trysts with Damian. Outsmarting January leads to an absurdly funny garden scene: May with Damian (snuck in past January) having sex up in a pear tree with January below thinking his wife has just gone in search of pears.

Like Alison in the "Miller's Tale," May is another young wife who betrays an old unappealing husband. Phillips writes:

> The resemblance of the *Merchant's Tale* garden to the Garden of Eden does not mean the tale depicts January's Fall from virtue to sin—January never was virtuous, even at the start of the tale. What the tale shows rather is people in a fallen state . . . the Fall it reveals is not one action in the plot . . . but [rather the Church teaching] that ever since Adam brought Original Sin into the world, humans had reproduced the Fall in their own daily lives "disobeying the illumination God sends through reason and conscience and succumbing to their lower powers of sensuality . . . and passion" (124).

The Squire's Tale

The Squire's tale is—appropriately—about a knight who arrives with a great flourish at a birthday feast celebrating the twenty-year reign of King Cambyuskan of Tartarye in Mongolia. The knight comes bearing gifts: for the king, a steed that will take him anywhere in a day; for his daughter, a mirror that foresees any coming misfortune, including a lover's treachery; and for all, a sword that pierces armor and heals wounds. The tale has confusing stops and starts, but there is an exquisite scene of the daughter comforting a female falcon. With the king's help she has learned her lover has betrayed her.

The Franklin's Tale

The Franklin tells a Breton lay—a short story in verse about a romantic adventure or a supernatural event. It is another of the marriage tales. A French knight, Arveragus, leaves his beloved wife, Dorigen, alone for two years while he performs knightly duties in England. With fear in her heart that her husband on his return will be shipwrecked on the dangerous rocks of Brittany's coastline, Dorigen delicately chides God for creating them and then asks a lovesick squire to remove them in exchange for her love. The squire petitions Apollo to make the rocks seem to disappear by raising the water in the ocean. Apollo consents and Dorigen, in shock over the dreadful dilemma she has created for herself, cites for Fortuna, twenty-two women in the same situation who killed themselves. In her study of Chaucerian humor, Jean E. Jost cites this tale for evincing one variation of that humor she names "Joy Following Woe":

> The conclusion [of this tale] is unambiguously happy, for unlike the previous serious comedic tales, this tale depicts no one injuring or taking advantage of another. By kindness and generosity, an harmonious resolution satisfies both characters and audience in a comedic and joyful victory. (Jost, xxxi)

The Doctor of Medicine's Tale

The doctor takes his tale from Livy's history of Rome and gives it a disturbing rendition. The tale is nobody's favorite, and how it could be construed as entertaining or instructive is unclear to many readers.

The story is a grim re-enactment of the parental sacrifice of a child ritual, evocative of God's commandment to Abraham that he slay his son Isaac. But only a code of human honor, not a divine order, has power here. Virginia, only child of Sir Virginius, catches the lecherous attention of Apius, a judge and ruler of the region. He devises a false charge against Virginius and orders that Virginia be surrendered to him as punishment. Virginius, facing an unthinkable dilemma, informs his daughter and gives her a choice: death or shameful submission to Apius.

Lengthy descriptions of Virginia's beauty and virtue make these scenes especially unbearable to contemplate. She chooses death "as gentle as possible" and is beheaded by her father. Apius, as "reward," receives her head and condemns Virginius to death by hanging. Virginius is rescued by his fellow citizens and it is Apius, thrown in jail, who dies by his own hand.

In horror, this tale matches that of the little martyred boy told by the Prioress, and the Host curses it ("God's nails and blood, alas, poor maid"). He then condemns to death all lawyers who abuse their trade and informs the doctor that his tale has given him "heart-disease." He pleads with the Pardoner to tell a cheerful tale. The Pardoner agrees but wants to get drunk first. The pilgrims express fear that the Pardoner's tale will be a dirty joke.

The Pardoner's Tale

Before he begins, the Pardoner, whom we know from the *Prologue* to be a deceitful scoundrel, explains his preaching practices. He proudly boasts of flaunting the papal seal he carries to grant pardons, selling "relics" he promises will cure farm animals from snake bites, taking money from the poor to fund his numerous pleasures, and cleverly speaking Latin—"Radix malorum est cupiditas" ("Greed is the root of all evil")—probably the only Church Latin he has learned, and certainly not for putting any constraints on his own activities. Despite his own blatant amorality ("Why copy the Apostles?"), the Pardoner seems pleased to offer an "exemplum"—a tale with a moral.

The Pardoner describes a company of young men gleefully pursuing all manner of "vice and ribaldry"—activities with which he has just confessed his own familiarity. Although his theme is greed, he gets distracted by "sins of the tavern"— mainly drunkenness—and gives examples of the ill deeds done mistakenly under its influence. Lot, for example, was too drunk to know he was sleeping with his own daughters, and King Herod, drunk at a feast, ordered the murder of John the Baptist.

Returning to his story, the Pardoner tells about three carousing youths who hear a "hand-bell clink before a coffin going to a grove." This sound they take as a sign that a friend has been slain. It is here that Chaucer makes his only mention of the Plague and its recurring decimation of whole populations: a "privy [secret] thief [men] call Death." Like Lot and Herod before them, the three companions make an especially foolhardy choice. On "God's blessed bones," they vow to join forces and slay the traitor "Death": "If we can only catch his, Death is dead!"

A half mile into their mission, they come across an old man and rudely taunt him. The man stands his ground and cryptically explains his own mission to find someone who "would change his youth to have my age," or, failing that, to find death itself—"an opening in Mother Earth for himself." Brashness of youth combined with intoxication renders the young men incapable of compassion for the old man or even of understanding that for the old and infirm Death may not be an enemy. Their failure of imagination will lead to a stark irony: the old man they shamelessly mistreat will still be alive after they are dead.

The old man directs them to Death's residence; when they arrive they discover eight bushels of gold coins, divisible by two but not by three. They lose interest in their quest and two stay to guard their treasure and send off the third to buy wine and bread. In his absence they agree to murder their younger companion on his return and divide the coins between them. (Wasn't there enough already? Had not this fortune just fallen on them undeservedly and gratuitously?) The youngest has fallen prey to a similar greed; he adds a "kernel" of rat poison to two of the three bottles. Bread and poisoned wine: a perversion of the Last Supper.

Three things happen next, one unexpected, one highly humorous, and one outrageous. The Pardoner reveals that he believes in the authenticity of the pardons Christ offers but not the ones he pretends to give. This makes him a sinner who continues sinning knowing he will be sent to Hell for his sins. Then he makes a show of promising not to deceive the pilgrims and offers on the spot to sell them relics for their protection in case misfortune should befall them on the trip. The Host cannot abide this brazen spectacle (he's been the first asked to pay up). Apoplectic, he curses in the rudest of ways that he would, if he could, separate the Pardoner from his own testicles and enshrine them in hog feces. A worse curse is hard to imagine or a more comically tumultuous scene. The Knight, traditional keeper of social order, must once again intervene. Rather miraculously, he gets the Pardoner, struck dumb with anger, and the Host, invective flowing like froth from his mouth, to calm down enough to share an embrace that ends the tale.

The Second Nun's Tale

The nameless Nun riding with the Prioress begins by warning that faith without works is futile ("Talk the talk and walk the walk"). Hers—a saint's tale—recounts the life of Cecelia whose church in Rome still stands. Cecelia seeks to convert her husband and others to Christianity, and because she is successful, she is brought before a judge who orders her execution. She miraculously survives three strikes of the executioner's blade and in her three remaining days of life, she gives away her possessions and establishes a church. After her death, she is made a saint by the pope

The Canon's Yeoman's Tale

Five miles from Canterbury something new and dramatic occurs: the Pilgrims are overtaken by two newcomers—a Canon and a Yeoman, both alchemists—who want to join their company. The Canon flees because he wants their illicit trade kept secret and the yeoman stays to reveal it. Part One of the tale describes his seven years with the Canon and some technical details about how they ply their trade. It's a dangerous business: we hear about a "wall-splitting" explosion that flings an iron pot and its alchemical contents in all directions. "All that glitters is not gold," he warns. Part Two provides details of one instance of alchemical trickery practiced by a corrupt Canon.

The Manciple's Tale

The Cook has fallen asleep on his horse from too much drink. Awakened by the Host to tell a tale, he can barely speak and the Manciple steps in to help. When the Manciple gets a look at the Cook's drunken countenance and smells his "cursed breath," he hurls insults at him. The exasperated Cook flails about until he loses balance and falls off his horse. Chaucer could have stopped here (it's not even the Cook's tale; he's already told his) and the scene would have been funny enough, but his comic spirit must have been irrepressible because he gives his Narrator a few more lines about the Cook sprawled on the ground:

Fine cavalry performance for a cook!
Pity he couldn't have held on by his ladle.
They got him back at last into the cradle
After a great deal of shoving to and fro
To lift him up was a sorry show;
Poor, pallid soul, unwieldier than most!

The Manciple's tale is about Apollo's white crow that could imitate human speech and also sing. Apollo's wife takes a lover when he's not looking, but the crow reveals the treachery. The enraged husband kills his wife and punishes the crow by decreeing that from now on crows will be black and unable to speak or sing. The Manciple ends his cautionary tale with this warning: "Refrain your tongue and think upon the crow."

The Parson's Tale

At day's end, the Parson speaks last, and, with the Knight at the beginning, encloses the tales in a framework of noble service and humble reverence before God. His tale is distinctive in being neither funny nor fictional; indeed, the Parson may startle the reader with his rejection of stories altogether, favoring, he says, what Saint Paul called "truth." His "tale" is a sermon that informs and instructs: informs about mortal and venial sins; and instructs about how to find contrition in one's heart and prepare to make the final confession of the day and of one's life.

After a day spent telling and listening to tales about all manner of sinful behaviors, it is gratifying to hear the Parson remind everyone that God, with infinite generosity, desires and provides for the salvation of every human being. The sermon may also influence readers who have absorbed the sermon's teaching and are eager to get right back into life to re-write their own stories more aligned with its message.

Critical Views

G.K. CHESTERTON ON CHAUCER'S GREATNESS

The medieval word for a Poet was a Maker, which indeed is
the original meaning of a Poet. . . . There was never a man
who was more of a Maker than Chaucer. He made a national
language; he came very near to making a nation. At least
without him it would probably never have been either so fine
a language or so great a nation. Shakespeare and Milton were
the greatest sons of their country; but Chaucer was the Father
of his Country, rather in the style of George Washington.
And apart from that, he made something that has altered
all Europe more than the Newspaper: the Novel. He was a
novelist when there were no novels. I mean by the novel the
narrative that is not primarily an anecdote or an allegory, but
is valued because of the almost accidental variety of actual
human characters. The Prologue of *The Canterbury Tales* is
the Prologue of Modern Fiction. . . . The astonishing thing is
not so much that an Englishman did this as that Englishmen
hardly ever brag about it. Nobody waves a Union Jack and
cries, 'England made jolly stories for the whole earth.' It is
not too much to say that Chaucer made not only a new nation
but a new world; and was none the less its real maker because
it is an unreal world. And he did it in a language that was
hardly usable until he used it; and to the glory of a nation that
had hardly existed till he made it glorious. . . .

Now even if we consider Chaucer only as a humorist, he
was in this very exact sense a great humorist. And by this I
do not only mean a very good humorist. I mean a humorist
in the grand style; a humorist whose broad outlook embraced
the world as a whole, and saw even great humanity against a
background of greater things. . . .

The Poet is the Maker; he is the creator of a cosmos; and
Chaucer is the creator of the whole world of his creatures. He
made the pilgrimage; he made the pilgrims. He made all the
tales that are told by the pilgrims. Out of him is all the golden

pageantry and chivalry of the Knight's Tale; all the rank and rowdy farce of the Miller's; he told through the mouth of the Prioress the pathetic legend of the Child Martyr and through the mouth of the Squire the wild, almost Arabian romance of Cambuscan. And he told them all in sustained melodious verse, seldom so continuously prolonged in literature; in a style that sings from start to finish. Then in due course, as the poet is also a pilgrim among the other pilgrims, he is asked for his contribution. He is at first struck dumb with embarrassment: and then suddenly starts a gabble of the worst doggerel in the book. It is so bad that, after a page or two of it, . . . [t]he poet is shouted down by a righteous revolt of his hearers, and can only defend himself by saying sadly that this is the only poem he knows. Then, by way of a final climax or anticlimax of the same satire, he solemnly proceeds to tell a rather dull story *in prose*.

Now a joke of that scale goes a great deal beyond the particular point, or pointlessness, of *The Rime of Sir Topas*. Chaucer is mocking not merely bad poets but good poets; the best poet he knows; 'the best in this kind are but shadows.' Chaucer, having to represent himself as reciting bad verse, did very probably take the opportunity of parodying somebody else's bad verse. But the parody is not the point. The point is in the admirable irony of the whole conception of the dumb or doggerel rhymer who is nevertheless the author of all the other rhymes; nay, even the author of their authors. Among all the types and trades, the coarse miller, the hard-fisted reeve, the clerk, the cook, the shipman, the poet is the only man who knows no poetry. But the irony is wider and even deeper than that. There is in it some hint of those huge and abysmal ideas of which the poets are half-conscious when they write; the primal and elemental ideas connected with the very nature of creation and reality. It has in it something of the philosophy of a phenomenal world, and all that was meant by those sages, by no means pessimists, who have said that we are in a world of shadows. Chaucer has made a world of his own shadows, and, when he is on a certain plane, finds himself equally shadowy. It has in it all the mystery of the relation of the maker with things made. There falls on it from afar even some dark ray of the irony of God, who was mocked when He entered His own world, and killed when He came among His creatures.

ARTHUR W. HOFFMAN ON THE OPENING LINES OF THE PROLOGUE

In the opening lines of the Prologue springtime is characterized in terms of procreation, and a pilgrimage of people to Canterbury is just one of the many manifestations of the life thereby produced. The phallicism of the opening lines presents the impregnating of a female March by a male April, and a marriage of water and earth. The marriage is repeated and varied immediately as a fructifying of "bolt and heeth" by Zephirus, a marriage of air and earth. This mode of symbolism and these symbols as parts of a rite of spring have a long background of tradition; as Professor Cook[3] once pointed out, there are eminent passages of this sort in Aeschylus and Euripides, in Lucretius, in Virgil's *Georgics*, in Columella, and in the *Pervigilium Veneris*, and Professor Robinson cites Guido delle Colonne, Boccaccio, Petrarch, and Boethius. Zephirus is the only overt mythological figure in Chaucer's passage, but, in view of the instigative role generally assigned to Aphrodite in the rite of spring, she is perhaps to be recognized here, as Professor Cook suggested, in the name of April, which was her month both by traditional association and by one of the two ancient etymologies.[4] Out of this contest of the quickening of the earth presented naturally and symbolically in the broadest terms, the Prologue comes to pilgrimage and treats pilgrimage first as an event in the calendar of nature, one aspect of the general springtime surge of human energy and longing. There are the attendant suggestions of the renewal of human mobility after the rigor and confinement of winter, the revival of wayfaring now that the ways are open. The horizon extends to distant shrines and foreign lands, and the attraction of the strange and faraway is included before the vision narrows and focusses upon its English specifications and the pilgrimage to the shrine at Canterbury with the vows and gratitude that send pilgrims there. One way of regarding the structure of this opening Passage would emphasize the magnificent progression from the broadest inclusive generality to the firmest English specification, from the whole western tradition of the celebration of spring (including, as Cook pointed out, such a non-English or very doubtfully English detail as "the droghte of March") to a local event of English society and English Christendom, from natural forces in their most general operation to a very specific and Christian manifestation of those forces. And yet one may regard the structure in another way, too; if, in the calendar of nature, the passage moves from general to particular, does it not, in the calendar of piety, move from nature to something that includes and oversees nature? Does not the passage move from an activity naturally generated and impelled to a governed activity, from force to *telos*? Does not the passage move from Aphrodite and *amor* in their secular operation to the sacred embrace of "the hooly blisful martir" and of *amor dei*?

The transition from nature to supernature is emphasized by the contrast between the healthful physical vigor of the opening lines and the reference to sickness that appears in line 18. On the one hand, it is physical vitality which conditions the pilgrimage; on the other hand, sickness occasions pilgrimage. It is, in fact, rather startling to come upon the word "seeke" at the end of this opening passage, because it is like a breath of winter across the landscape of spring. "Whan that they were seeke" may, of course, refer literally to illnesses of the winter just past, but, in any event, illness belongs symbolically to the inclement season. There is also, however, a strong parallelism between the beginning and end of this passage, a parallelism that has to do with restorative power. The physical vitality of the opening is presented as restorative of the dry earth; the power of the saint is presented as restorative of the sick. The seasonal restoration of nature parallels a supernatural kind of restoration that knows no season; the supernatural kind of restoration invokes a wielding and directing of the forces of nature. The Prologue begins, then, by presenting a double view of the Canterbury pilgrimage: the pilgrimage is one tiny manifestation of a huge tide of life, but then, too, the tide of life ebbs and flows in response to the power which the pilgrimage acknowledges, the power symbolized by "the hooly blisful martir."

Notes

3. Albert S. Cook, "Chaucerian Papers—Prologue—I:1, 1–11." *Transactions of the Connecticut Academy of Arts and Sciences*, XXIII (New Haven, 1919), pp. 5–21.

4. Cook, pp. 5–10.

E.T. DONALDSON ON CHAUCER THE POET AND PILGRIM

If one imagines Chaucer himself reading the *Canterbury Tales* at court—as it is likely that he did—one can begin to see some of the elements that make up this complex poetic vision. In the first place, Chaucer obviously exploits his physical personality—that of a pleasingly plump, cheerful, perhaps unimpressive little man—for such humor as it will afford: he assigns this personality to his fictional representative in such a way that when it is mentioned within the poem the audience will laugh at it as they probably never would at the actual Chaucer. But the physical similarity between the two Chaucers is ultimately less important than the temperamental similarity which it is meant to suggest—the affability, the air of deference, of eagerness to please, of naïveté, all of them somehow exaggerated when the man they belong to puts them into his fictional surrogate. The temperamental similarity is in turn chiefly important as a device that serves to bring out the more significant mental dissimilarity between Chaucer the poet and Chaucer the narrator. It is here that the latter takes leave of the former, for while the narrator is almost unfailingly simple-minded, the poet who has created him and has found a place for his simplicity in the poem—indeed, has sometimes made the meaning depend on it—is anything but simple-minded. . . .

The pilgrim Chaucer is, in his own unpretentious way, a seeker after truth. . . . But our pilgrim's way of proceeding on his quest reveals from the very beginning a fatal overconfidence in his ability to see things as they are merely by looking at them hard. To be sure, he is energetic, does not trust to luck, and makes a valiant show of braving experience. It is with a distinct hint of pride that he reports on his success in interviewing all nine and twenty of his fellow pilgrims before sunset; it is with rugged determination that he promises to relate all he knows concerning every single one of them. But he never stops to consider whether the intentions of a conscientious reporter are enough to insure an accurate presentation of reality. . . .

The simple equations by means of which Chaucer is attempting to keep a record of his memorable experiences on the way to Canterbury are constantly breaking down.

The break-down occurs, of course, on a larger scale as well, and it is in this way that the ironic role of Chaucer the pilgrim is amplified in proportion as his control over his material decreases. In the context of the Prologue, whole portraits get out of hand, and can be read upside down, as it were. The Monk's is an excellent example: almost everything that is said in praise of him as a manly man can reflect unfavorably on his supposedly chosen vocation as a monk. In the context of the entire poem, the pilgrim Chaucer's own tale of Sir Thopas gets out of hand, and is publicly censored as unworthy of continuation. We, who in the absence of evidence to the contrary had originally extended to the fictional "I" the willing suspension of our own disbelief, must learn to look for guidance to the poet Chaucer, trusting that he and the pilgrim are not by any means identical in all respects.

Apart from humor, and an implied compliment to the sophisticated intelligence of the audience, what has been gained, one may ask, by the poet's considered refusal to speak directly, in his own person? The way of indirection is generally the way of irony, and allows for a pervasive suggestiveness to which the reader is then free to assign any number of meanings. Irony, moreover, provides in both tone and content for the possibility of a sustained paradox. Medieval literature abounds in satire, not infrequently full of savage condemnation. Chaucer's satire, by and large, is far funnier than the rest, and yet partly for this reason perhaps more telling. The narrator's failure to see what is wrong emphasizes the wrong; irony, of which this is a complex kind, always heightens. Yet a satiric portrait, while intellectually telling, need not, thanks to the narrator's good nature, be emotionally scathing. This is not the only way to write successful satire, but it was clearly Chaucer's intention to write satire of a rather special kind; to present both halves of the human paradox and to retain both without allowing the positive and negative values to cancel each other out. The Monk as monk is a failure who must surely be condemned by discriminating men. As a man, the Monk is one of the most impressive of God's creatures and his manliness, although irrelevant to his vocation, commands the appreciation of men. The narrator's undiscriminating attitude ironically condemns, literally appreciates.

And Chaucer the poet, on whom not only Chaucer the pilgrim, but also the Host and the Parson depend for insight? He, too, is a pilgrim, and exemplifies yet another aspect of man's search for truth. His vision of human reality postulates the simultaneous existence of at first sight mutually exclusive opposites, and is almost perfectly contained in Pope's famous couplet on man:

Sole judge of Truth, in endless Error hurled:
The glory, jest, and riddle of the world.

PAUL G. RUGGIERS ON CHAUCERIAN COMEDY

We will make a distinction at the outset that is obvious to everyone but needs to be set forth early: (a) Half of the comic tales are about conflicts in which the reprisal is a sexual triumph over a conventional, older person. Of these tales, i.e., those of the Miller, Reeve, Merchant, and Shipman, only the *Shipman's Tale* does not tell us about the relative ages of the agents except to imply by the age of the Monk the general age of all; (b) Half of the tales, those of the Friar, Pardoner, Summoner, and Canon's Yeoman, are nonsexual tales, comedies without lighthearted humor; these are, more frankly, unmaskings. They each have some quality of the sinister about them that raises ethical considerations in a way that the first group does not; they describe ugly actions in the process of raising questions about the kind of society that allows them. They are comedies that frankly face up to human concerns: good and evil, life and death. The comedies about adultery, it should be pointed out, may also raise criticisms of a society that tolerates the marriage of youth and age; the *Shipman's Tale*, for example, or the *Merchant's Tale*, both have the capacity to challenge us at levels we have not anticipated. Seriousness is always an implied quality in Chaucerian comedy.

In both types of comedy, the whole tendency of Chaucerian comedy is to move from an old law, stated at the outset (usually as an enchaining marriage or family order in the tales of the Miller, Reeve, Merchant, and Shipman), to a wily escape from its bondage into momentary freedom from its constraints; or in the darker comedies (those of the Friar, the Summoner, the Pardoner, and the Canon's Yeoman's Introduction) to tear away illusion and hypocrisy by building the *agon*, not around the opposition of youth and age, but around demonstrations of conspiratorial behavior destined to be exposed as hypocritical, thievish, or mendacious.

These two types are quite different in their emphasis, the first kind being aimed largely at giving satisfaction through cleverly arranged episodes, suspense, and a sense of something being carefully nudged toward surprise and an unexpected conflation of happenings, like the episode of the misplaced cradle in the *Reeve's Tale*, or the cry of "water, water" in the *Miller's Tale*, which tops all previous surprises. The closing barrage of puns at the conclusion of the *Shipman's Tale* enables the level of comic statement to soar immediately into the dimensions of verbal wit.

In the second kind of tale (those of Friar, Summoner, Pardoner, and Canon's Yeoman), the emphasis is largely upon describing the ethos of a society or group: something more communal, perhaps a community of demon types, mostly hypocrites and liars, persons wearing masks of one sort or another, who are either exposed or destroyed. In the *Pardoner's Tale*, for example, in the enveloping sermon a scapegoat is made by his own words to unmask himself and to undergo the threat of expulsion (only to be restored in Chaucer's comic generosity); and similarly in the exemplum, the three rioters, one of whom serves as a scapegoat, get what they deserve, being shown as thieves and murderers. It might be noted that the figure of a scapegoat may make for pathos—a mood that Chaucer manages to avoid here—which can destroy the comic tone if carried too far.[5] . . .

The distinction that may be made between the two kinds of comic structures has to do with a deeper, more serious view of things, a willingness to make comparison between higher and lower norms in the manner of satire and irony. Both types of tales yield their special satisfactions: the closed garden of the *Merchant's Tale* has been successfully invaded, the upward mobility of the Reeve's snobbish family has been damaged, the unwise marriage of unlikes in the *Miller's* and *Merchant's* tales has been given its "just" due and the guileless simplicity of the merchant of the *Shipman's Tale* has been confirmed (but he seems no worse off than before; the other characters seem faintly shameful). In the others, perhaps because of their stronger moral and social concerns, the satisfaction derives from seeing conventions, theological and moral, vindicated.

A writer who vindicates or defends piously held beliefs is writing comedies of a limited range; but they are not to be dispraised for being so. For the Christian poet, stripping off the disguises and masks of villainy precisely in terms of religiously defined norms and writing comedies about damnation demonstrates that comedy may derive its materials from anywhere; attitude and tone are all. And obviously comedy does not exclude suffering; it makes capital of it but uses it for its own ends and with the right tone and attitude.

These two broad types of comedic structures in Chaucer thus confirm that double perspective which is implicit in comedy generally. One cannot know the merely existing without testing it against essence, the factual without the ideal, the life of instinct without the life of reason, body without soul. The norms which are vindicated in Chaucer's comedies about adultery are clearly those of nature; in the others, the tension is clearer in terms of good and evil men and women. Chaucer does not pretend that his protagonists are not bad men and women; they are shown to be so, and one has the feeling that their predictable destruction has been part of a larger justification of law.

Chance, trickery, and improbable possibilities may be the laws of the first kind or comedies; from the perspective of the other type, these laws dwindle before an inexorable law. In the first type, things turn out well for the agents; in the second, for the audience.

Note

5. Elder Olson, *The Theory of Comedy* (Indiana University Press, pp. 52–54. It happens that these two classes of tales jibe loosely with a part of the scheme evolved by Olson for dramatic forms. The second group represent his "plots of folly . . . in which the agent acts in error," for whatever reason; the first group corresponds to his "plots of cleverness . . . in which the stratagems of the agent produce the comic action." The agents are rewarded or punished according to their deserts; according as the agent is well- or ill-intentioned, we respond. The agents themselves, those that fall into the class of the ridiculous, may be of three types: (a) morally sound but intellectually deficient; (b) morally deficient but clever; and (c) deficient both intellectually and morally. Moreover, the agents may act from good or bad motives.

Olson's scheme, illustrated from a simple archetype (p. 53), is as follows:

Plots of Folly: well-intentioned fool;
outcome must be successful.
Plots of Folly: ill-intentioned fool;
outcome must be failure.
Plots of Cleverness: well-intentioned cleverman;
outcome must be successful.
Plots of Cleverness: ill-intentioned cleverman;
outcome must be failure.

In this scheme the friar of the *Summoner's Tale*, the summoner of the *Friar's Tale*, the three rioters of the *Pardoner's Tale*, and the Canon of the *Canon's Yeoman's Tale* may be seen as ill-intentioned fools, for whom the outcome must be failure; in the cleverness plots, the wife and monk of the *Shipman's Tale*, the pairs of young men in the Miller's and Reeve's tales, Damian and May of the *Merchant's Tale*, because they succeed in their various ways, must—to preserve the scheme—be seen as well-intentioned. This constitutes a definition of terms that strains our belief in the applicability of the theory to Chaucer's tales. Obviously much hangs upon our definition of "well-intentioned." One has to adopt a rather special perspective to see the agents in this light, that is, as well-intentioned with reference exclusively to their own interests.

V.A. KOLVE ON CHAUCER'S FABLIAUX

Chaucer warns that what is to follow is a "cherles tale" in which "harlotrie" is "tolden," he raises in his audience certain expectations and dismisses others, addressing their prior literary experience as something he will confirm or revise in the course of the tale. For the sake of convenience I shall call the genre "fabliau," though I do not mean to restrict the term to tales derived solely from the French tradition; many of the Italian *novelle*, especially Boccaccio's, imply a similar set of propositions about human experience, and that set as such is our present concern. In writing his "cherles tales," Chaucer drew upon both French and Italian sources, and for our present purposes we may likewise ignore distinctions of provenance in favor of the assumptions—the vision of life—they share.

Characters in such stories live, for the most part, as though no moral imperatives existed beyond those intrinsic to the moment. They inhabit a world of cause and effect, pragmatic error and pragmatic punishment, that admits no goals beyond self-gratification, revenge, or social laughter—the comedic celebration of any selfishness clever enough to succeed. The exclusions of the genre are as decisive as its preferences, chief among them the fact that no one—not the characters, not the author, not the person whom the reader or auditor is invited to think of himself as being—apprehends the action "under the aspect of eternity," in terms of good and evil, heaven or hell. If religious matters intrude, they are more likely to do so as a comic means of manipulation than as an adumbration of the divine. The end sought is laughter, not meditation on a countertruth. The actions are swift, the stories short, and there is little room for detailed characterization: a person is what he does, and one or two actions tell us all we will ever learn about him; for the rest, there is only his membership, already real or (by the end of the tale) at last begun, in a company of more or less grown-up people. The company is made up of familiar types—avaricious merchants, restless wives, suspicious husbands, bragging cowards, lecherous priests, clever clerks—all of them persons who have traveled a certain distance down life's road, show some dust from the journey, and are able to assimilate a further lesson or two without too serious a loss of social composure. In this world of winner and loser, duper and duped, life is a compromising business; it is no great shock to discover, in the course of the action, yet another way in which a person can use or be used.

The generic introduction to this "cherles tale" is meant to free Chaucer's art from certain demands we elsewhere legitimately make upon it. But, as we soon discover, he means nothing reductive thereby. In every one of his fabliaux—I include in this group the tales of the Miller, Reeve, Shipman, Summoner, and Merchant—Chaucer gives us more than the genre promises, or than most other examples had ever thought to provide. In the case of the Miller's Tale, we are offered not only the essential vision of truth that defines the genre—a fiercely comic respect for things as they are and for the way folly will find its own punishment—but something imaginatively finer besides. Working with three fabliau motifs of a highly volatile kind—two of them coarsely obscene (the misdirected kiss and the arse branding) and a third that verges upon blasphemy (the parodic reenactment of Noah's Flood)—Chaucer manages to create a narrative that is not only funny but also oddly innocent and imaginatively gay. The Miller's Tale represents the fabliau largely denatured of its indecency, brusqueness, and cynicism, although it recounts an action as outrageous as any in the entire corpus of such tales.

That of course is the work of a storyteller who is also a stylist, a rhetorician exploring the furthest possibilities of a genre.

ALCUIN BLAMIRES ON EXCESS AND RESTRAINT IN THE *TALES*

In the *General Prologue* we find the pilgrim Chaucer applying for a licence to introduce all manner of audacities, under pretext that, if he is to record the speech and behaviour of the pilgrims accurately (never mind that his *alter ego* is composing them), he must reproduce even their broadest language: for, 'Whoso shal telle a tale after a man, . . . He may nat spare, although he were his brother' [731–7]. This licence for 'not sparing' (not holding back) is tantamount to a *carte blanche* for Chaucer's storytellers to express themselves with colourful and provocative intensity. It is tantamount to an ingenious excuse for suspending literary decorum and allowing speakers to let rip, exhibiting either themselves or those they scorn as daringly as the poet wishes.

I suppose the two most virtuoso exhibitions are those of the Pardoner and the Wife of Bath. . . . Each seems constructed to court audience shock or outrage, as if out of some compulsive bravado. Thus the Pardoner brazenly exhibits such extravagances as his vicious determination to extract money or provisions from the poorest widow even if her children should consequently die of hunger [*Pardoner's Prologue*, 448–51].

The Wife's brash disclosures arise, she claims, out of all 'entente . . . to pleye' and out of her 'fantasye' (here probably 'whim' or 'fancy', but it is a suggestive word as we shall see [*Wife of Bath's Prologue*, 189–92]). However, she is also egged on, interestingly enough, by fellow-exhibitionist the Pardoner, who after interrupting prods her, 'Telle forth youre tale, spareth for no man' [186]. She hardly needs his encouragement. Arch-scourge of men, she revels in her shrill account of the incessant scolding by which she subjugated her first three husbands. She 'wolde nat spare hem' (restrain her campaign against them),

80

not even if the Pope himself had sat beside them at the supper-table, as she puts it with glorious hyperbole [420–1].

These examples perhaps suggest that the strategy of no-holds-barred audacity yields effects which are lifelike precisely because they are larger than life. They manifest the sharp-etched quality of a cartoon, whether entertainingly (the Wife) or disturbingly (the Pardoner). 'Not-sparing' implies that the normally unsayable will get said with vivid candour, as indeed happens in the best cartoons. Chaucer presses as it were a 'release' button in such cases, triggering his most colourfully mischievous or satirical creativity. . . .

Self-restraint is also endangered by *fantasie*, whose presence in the *Tales* we are now to consider. *Fantasie* has a slightly more technical sense for Chaucer than its modern equivalent. It denotes the domination of a person's thought by often delusive (but not necessarily 'fantastic') images or ideas; a sort of mental obsession indulged to the detriment of objectivity. Chaucer keenly develops narrative opportunities for exploring *fantasie*, since this is another means of heightening his poetry and taking us to the more spectacular extremities of human behaviour. . . .

The chief exemplars of absorbed reverie are, naturally enough, the various courtly suitors in the tales. Chaucer sustains the medieval literary convention that a male lover, once smitten with the 'arrows' of' beauty, nurses an all-consuming image of the beloved in an agony of secretive fear and frustration. According to the *Knight's Tale*, in acute cases this locked-in obsession produces a mental malfunction as serious as the 'mania' caused when fluids of Melancholy invade the imaginative portion of the brain (the 'celle fantastik' [1372–6]). Here we have a poker-faced clinical diagnosis, one of the gambits by which Chaucer, even while committing much poetic energy to love's subjective pathos, sustains our objectivity towards it. Other gambits, both of which feature in the *Knight's Tale*, are to modulate from lyricism into wholesome mockery of the lover's eccentric moodiness—up one minute and down the next like a bucket in a well [1528–33]; and to operate equivocally on the very limits of acceptable hyperbole when expressing the lover's languishings, tears, swoons, and his lurid talk of death.

For Chaucer, then, the courtly lover is an inevitable focus of extravagance. Possessed by ungovernable emotions, the lover will commit actions which are 'heigh folye' by the standards of mature rational consideration [1798]. Thus Arcite risks his neck in returning from the safety of Thebes to Athens (where he is outlawed), but declares 'for the drede of death shal I nat spare / To se my lady' [1395–7 (i.e. not refrain from seeing her)]. We realise that there is an 'unsparing' dimension in love, too. Aurelius demonstrates it again in the *Franklin's Tale*. He would give the whole world, let alone the gigantic sum that an Orleans magician demands, to win Dorigen [1226–9]. And, if Dorigen in her *fantasie* suffers a 'rage' of grief, Aurelius matches her, after hearing her verdict on his love-plea, with all intensity of self-torturing sorrow that reduces him to near-insane 'ravying' [1026–7] and thence to a two-year trance 'in langour and in torment furvus' [1101–2]. . . .

We could take up many more pages analyzing self-restraint and self-control in Chaucer's poem. Paradoxically, he sometimes develops them in extravagant vein, too, as in the case of Griselda in the *Clerk's Tale*. He 'etches' her hyper-controlled behaviour as daringly as he ever etches the uncontrolled mentality elsewhere.

Our conclusion must be that Chaucer explores human extravagance in triumphantly 'palpable' poetry, whose power to work upon our own imagination is enriched by the encompassing assurance that the intensities are wrought by a highly rational artist. I leave the reader to ponder therefore whether, of all the dualistic titles one might invent to express the cross-currents in this complex work, 'Excess and Restraint in *The Canterbury Tales*' would take us to the heart of the matter.

WINTHROP WETHERBEE ON THE ABSENCE OF ORDER

Chaucer goes to extraordinary lengths to show the obstacles to vision and knowledge posed by the pilgrims' existential situations, and we may compare his perspective to that of the great Franciscan philosopher of the previous generation, William of Ockham. "Ockham's razor" is often said to have severed philosophy from theology: this is an exaggeration, but his denial of the necessity of natural secondary causes (since there is nothing God might effect through a secondary cause that He is not equally able to accomplish directly), and his confinement of *scientia*, or real knowledge, to the sphere of observation and logical inference, tend in this direction. They allow us to affirm little about the relation of created life to God beyond the acknowledgment, through faith, of his omnipotence and goodness, and the ethical imperative of obeying his commands. Chaucer accepts similar constraints for his characters. Theseus' evocation of the benevolent "First Mover," insofar as it is more than a political gesture, is a leap of faith, and a pervasive concern of the *Tales* as a whole is the psychological effect of living with no more immediate confirmation of order and providence than such a leap provides. Some characters simply refuse to consider "Who hath the world in honde"; others reveal their anxiety in such neurotic forms as the Man of Law's vacillating attitude toward Providence or the Pardoner's compulsive blasphemy; and the Nun's Priest, apparently after serious thought, seems to have made peace with the likelihood that the large questions of providence and self-determination are unanswerable.

Cut off from a sure sense of relation to the divine, or of their place in a traditional hierarchy, the pilgrims question their own status. Many of the tales are essays in self-definition, attempts to establish values and goals that lead to startling revelations. The Knight, whose tale begins as an apology for chivalry, finds himself unable to bring it to a satisfying resolution, and is carried steadily toward a confrontation with the horror of violence and death which challenges his chivalric values. The Wife of Bath, trying to justify a life of striving for mastery in marriage, becomes half-aware that her deepest need is to be recognized and valued as a woman, something of which her society seems incapable. The Pardoner flaunts his success as a religious huckster and defies the taboo effect of his sexual abnormality, but gradually reveals a religious inner self that accepts the paradoxical guilt of the scapegoat, an agonizing display that illustrates the intolerance of a Christian society. In all these cases the tale-tellers' struggles are rendered more painful by a vision of order or harmony or forgiveness that seems to hover just out of reach.

ANNE LASKAYA ON CHAUCER AND COMPETITION

As a supreme ironist, Chaucer was fond of looking at any human value, belief, behavior, or emotion commonly exhibited in his culture from several different perspectives. Consequently, it is no wonder that we find him exploring the nature of masculine power and control, particularly calling attention to its achievements, its limitations, and its price. If . . . the desire for control is one pervasive feature of late medieval masculinity, inevitably Chaucer (the poet who studied human nature so closely) will include it in his portraits of male characters. And, indeed, tale after tale explores the extent of men's control over themselves, over others, and over the world around them. The *Tales* demonstrate that men who seek power over others inevitably run into conflict with one another; that is, that competition between men is an obvious consequence of men trying to realize, in their lives, a masculine identity based upon control. . . .

Clearly the conflicts between, say, the Miller and the Reeve or the Pardoner and the Summoner (even between the Parson and the Host) highlight the competition for power among the narrators themselves. Within the individual tales, too, competition among men often forms the basic dramatic tension for the plot. It is central to the contest between Palamon and Arcite in the *Knight's Tale*, to Nicholas, Absalon, and old John, the carpenter, in the *Miller's Tale*, to the tragedy of the *Physician's Tale*, to the greed played out in the *Pardoner's Tale*, to the conflict between the Fox and Chaunticleer in the *Nun's Priest's Tale*, and so on. Competition, in fact, forms the very occasion for the telling of the *Tales* when Harry Bailly, the pilgrims' host, initiates a storytelling contest. . . . This host proposes that the pilgrims pit their narrative talents against one another on their journey. For incentive, he promises a reward to the winner (the losers will pay for the winner's meal). He also promises punishment for anyone who refuses to cooperate or participate. The pilgrims approve the plan, making Harry the 'governour' who will judge the storytelling contest. They decide to be 'reuled . . . at his devys / In heigh and lough; and thus by oon assent,' they agree to be 'acorded to his juggement' (813–18). From the first moment of action on the journey, one man has established his authority over others and has shaped the others' experience; he has shaped it in the form of competition. Of course, the purpose here is entertainment, but the structure of the entertainment is competition. The comedy of the gaming situation establishes hierarchies of power and struggles for success and control which frame the *Tales*. In so far as the *Canterbury Tales* are grounded on the dynamic of competition, they are aligned with what the culture considers an aspect of the ideal masculine, at least in the heroic, courtly love, and intellectual traditions.

Perhaps it is not surprising that Chaucer would build his serial narrative on the dynamics of competition. Because the *Canterbury Tales* depict the process of telling a tale (each narrator taking us through this process again and again), one story the text itself tells is the story of storytelling; and there is a close affinity between competition, or the struggle to dominate, and the way Chaucer's narrators speak about creating narrative. We are frequently reminded that the storyteller must exert control over his or her tale. Each narrator must choose the tale he or she will tell, fashion its beginning, middle and end, select details, create syntax, rhythms, meters, and rhymes, and exert control over language, experience, characters, plot, and audience. Creating a tale involves the storyteller in a competitive relationship with disorder. Each narrator, like Harry Bailly, will set himself or herself up as governor and judge over all the elements in the story. What we see in the dynamics between Harry and the pilgrims is reenacted in the dynamics between author and text material.[2] Sometimes Harry has control; sometimes he does not. Sometimes narrators successfully shape and control their tales; sometimes tales get the best of their narrators. . . .

Situating the *Tales* at the site of competition carries with it several interesting critiques of the dominant medieval gender discourse. Of course, by placing his narrators within a competitive game, under the direction of a man, Chaucer reproduces the hierarchies of power which the dominant cultural discourse surrounding gender assumes: men will control. But, the subtleties lying potential in the choice of competition as the setting for the narratives do not always simply reinscribe the cultural discourse about men's rule. First of all, Chaucer's inclusion of women's voices in his storytelling competition suggests that, contrary to the ideals prescribed for women, competition is not just the purview of men. Whereas gender discourse in the Middle Ages encouraged men to compete, it did not encourage women to compete with men. Men were to control; women were to submit. Men were to speak; women were to be silent. Although they number far fewer than the men, the women in Chaucer's frame tale are not silent; they speak, much to our delight. They participate in the competitive game, openly competing with, and challenging, men—and they are not chastised for their participation. All the narrators, whether male or female, have equal opportunity to win the game. If the frame narrative suggests competition is not just a feature of relationships between men, but is also a feature of the relationships between men and women, it does not, however, depict overt competition between the women narrators. In so far as the Wife of Bath, the Prioress, and the Second Nun participate in the game, they compete with each other, but they never speak directly to one another as the male pilgrims do. Their tales are commented upon by men, surrounded by men's narratives, and told at the invitation of men. Whereas the frame narrative records overt conflict between male pilgrims, it nowhere dramatizes open conflict between women. The women compete primarily with men. At every immediate site of competition in the frame tale, men are always involved; women are not. Nevertheless, the inclusion of women's voices in the competition suggests that women need not be, nor are not, silent—that they can, and do, participate in the creation of narrative—and that they can be, and are, an active part of shaping the life of the community.

Note

2. Cf. Alan T. Gaylord, 'Sentence and Solaas in Fragment VII of the *Canterbury Tales*: Harry as Horseback Editor,' *PMLA* 82 (1967): 226–35.

DEREK BREWER ON THE MILLER'S TALE

The contrast between *The Miller's Tale* and *The Knight's Tale* is very refreshing, and very typical of Chaucer. Though not a parody of *The Knight's Tale*, it also tells of two young men in love with the same girl. . . .

The plot of *The Miller's Tale* is as fantastic as that of any romance. It is based on a common folktale: variants of the story are found in several languages. A young Oxford student lodging with an old roan tricks his simple-minded landlord, who has a young and beautiful wife, into believing that Noah's flood is coming again. So all three must spend the night in wooden tubs slung in the roof, in order safely to float out on the waters when need arises. The elderly husband falls asleep and the two young persons skip downstairs and into bed together. But along comes another lover of the wife, a fastidious, squeamish, village dandy. He serenades the wife and asks her for a kiss. The bedroom is on the ground floor, and she puts out her bottom which the unfortunate man kisses. It is a moment of awful comedy. He goes away in fury and returns with a red-hot piece of iron, a ploughshare. Again he serenades the wife. Her student-lover proposes to repeat the same exquisite joke, and puts out *his* bottom, and receives a jab from the burning-hot ploughshare; he withdraws with a scream of agony. To cool himself he shrieks for 'water!' The cry awakes the husband, who thinks the Flood has come and cuts the rope that holds his tub, and crashes to the floor, where he knocks himself out and breaks his arm. The wife and lover by their cries rouse their neighbours, and since many of these are students all take sides with the lover and tell the husband that he is mad, and laugh at him. Thus, he suffers, and the poem wastes no sympathy on him, concluding 'and thus his wife was seduced (though a blunter word is used), her lover scalded in the rear, and the dandy has kissed the lady's lower eye'.

I have told the story without names to emphasise how much the persons are roles or types: jealous old husband, lecherous student, lecherous village dandy, lecherous young wife. The wife is the centre of their attention, but the story is not about her: it is not even primarily about the men who circle round her as a sexual object: the story is, at its deepest or, as we may well say, at its lowest level, the articulation of a deliberately fantastic insult, common to all the languages of Europe, I should guess, in the Middle Ages; common even today, perhaps; the insult is the regrettable expression, 'Kiss my arse'. The insult is only funny in so far as coarse invective is funny, but there seems no doubt, to judge from the received history of comedy (as in the *Oxford Classical Dictionary*), that coarse invective is indeed the oldest form of humour. In the case of *The Miller's Tale*, however, the articulation of the insult into a fantastic story turns it into a classically comic structure; there is a reversal from top to bottom, if one may put it that way, yet in a context which prevents any tragic implications: the face-to-face human personal relationship of the kiss is grotesquely transformed, parodied and insulted; the spiritual or at any rate the emotional, imaginative, delicate, higher relationship of love is conquered by the grossly and disgustingly lower physical connection. Furthermore, the repetition of the first kiss by the burning second one produces further parody—we have all heard of burning kisses. And, of course, the further connection of the cry of 'water' brings down, lowers, the husband, in every sense. The very structure of the narrative is poetic. The story is a general lowering of the pretensions of the men; the wife never had any. In a way, it is a comic assertion of natural physical reality, though not of justice—an assertion of the reality of a young wife's natural lustfulness which is juxtaposed against the jealousy of a silly old man who would unrealistically restrain his wife, and against two deceitful and conceited young men, who want to exploit the wife's nature. We may well remember Aristotle's remark that comedy portrays people as worse than they usually are. Let us hope it is true. In origin the story is anti-feminist. All the men suffer: the woman unjustly escapes scot-free. The implication is that women trick men and make them suffer. But comedy is always ambivalent. And it always takes two to play the wife's game. So the story is not without sympathy for the wife. Chaucer is very sympathetic to women and he makes the wife very charming and attractive, though he mocks her too.

HELEN PHILLIPS ON INTENTIONAL DIVERSITY IN THE *TALES*

Surprising juxtapositions and variety are certainly the most obvious characteristics of the *Tales*. They are also the source of the most interesting critical questions the text asks. . . . The *Canterbury Tales* also offers great diversity of styles, moods and genres: from epic and religious lyric to parody.

The most challenging aspects of its diversity; however, are the conflicting moralities that seem to be present within the text, and the diversity of interpretation that Chaucer's writing invites. At times the narrative itself acts out multiple reader-response, by showing the pilgrims divided in their reactions or expectations concerning the tales they hear and tell. . . .

From his mixed band of pilgrims, varied in both their social status and their levels of morality, who are both the fictional narrators of his tales and a fictional audience, Chaucer creates a many-voiced narrative which lacks both the limitations and the safety of a single focalization.[3] The first-person narrator, the main narrator in one sense, does not organise the story-telling: the pilgrims themselves are given, in the fiction, control over the ordering and content of the series of tales; they quarrel about them and dispute authority. When the narrator does get to speak, they soon refuse to listen to what he has to say. In this way, and others, it is a polyphonic text: no one viewpoint is allowed to preside over the story-telling. . . . Chaucer's decision to paint his pilgrim company as a socially variegated group, full of rivalry and internal tensions has several different effects; it creates narratological complexities which intrigue the critic; it raises deep questions about the text's overall moral standpoint; and it could also be an image of Chaucer's awareness of his own late fourteenth-century context as a society of rapid economic and political change and movement, bringing classes into new relationships of rivalry and conflict, with challenges to established authority—from the rising power of the merchant classes, from the economic frustration and ambitions of artisans and peasants, and from discontent among reformers and laity about the state the Church. . . .

Diversity, then, is central to the *Tales* both on the obvious level of the social mix of the pilgrims and the range of genres, subjects, styles and moral seriousness in their stories, and also at a deeper level in the way the text permits disparate worldviews and incompatible readings to coexist, without subjugating them conclusively to one controlling vision, and the *Tales'* management of its dual impulses, towards unity and towards diversity, raises issues about how the multiplicity of human experience, desires and goals relates ultimately to the concept of a divine order. The variety in the *Canterbury Tales* thus presents us with some issues which are critical and others which are ultimately moral and theological questions about the design of human life and society. Politically the stance of the *Tales* may seem at first conservative or apolitical, serving the interests of the ruling class for whom, and among whom, Chaucer worked as a courtier and civil servant, and yet subversive forces and problematic elements are also discernibly present in most of the tales to a degree it is hard for the critic to ignore, and the whole miscellany of narratives, juxtaposed with each other, ensures that no single tale can create its own world of values without being challenged by the often incompatible values of other tales around it. The vulgarity; lawlessness and celebration of physical pleasure in the *Miller's*

Tale is not accommodated in any way—by anything within the fictional narrative of the *Tales*—to the very different values of the *Knight's Tale*, which precedes it; similarly, the Man of Law's condemnation of the miseries of poverty in his Prologue contrasts completely with the praise of poverty as a spiritually and even practically advantageous state expressed in the *Wife of Bath's Tale*. Nothing in the titles provides any way of reconciling the two. In his company of pilgrims, brought together both by holiday spirit and by religious purpose, Chaucer creates an appropriately dialectic frame for the stories: a chattering and quarrelling assembly of *diverse folk* with diverse reactions, who comment on the tales they tell and hear, and offer a bewildering variety of interpretations and assumptions about their purpose and meaning during the so-called 'link' passages of pilgrim conversation between tales, thus foregrounding for the critic the issue of individual reader-response to literature and its meaning(s).

Note
3. Focalization is the stance or point of view from which a text seems to be written, whether this is explicit (a named narrator with a specific personality and life-experience, for example) or implicit (a set of attitudes, perceptions and assumptions which underlie the ways in which the narrative presents material to the reader. An example of very strong single focalization is John Buchan's *The Thirty-Nine Steps*, which is localized, explicitly and implicitly, through the perceptions and attitudes of Richard Hannay, its first-person narrator.

JOHN C. HIRSH ON LOVE AND DEATH IN
THE KNIGHT'S TALE

Christopher Daniell's *Death and Burial in Medieval England*[1] . . . shows the pervasiveness of the topic, and the multitude of ways in which medieval persons addressed it. What stands out, both in Daniell and in Chaucer, is the public role death assumed, the almost easy place it held in everyday discourse. . . .

Daniell points out that the recent excavation of a medieval graveyard at Taunton showed that no women buried there had lived beyond age 45, and that the "most likely age to die" (133) was between 25 and 30, and then 30–35, but that those who reached 50 "were likely to live much longer" (134). . . .

It is thus not surprising that, as soon as we escape from the idealized realism of the General Prologue, we encounter death, sudden, undeserved, and with dramatic social implications. . . . [The] *Knight's Tale* is deeply concerned with love and . . . with death, indeed love and death seem often to run together in Chaucer's mind, as in so much Western literature generally. When we look at the tale as a whole, the links appear clearly. . . . In an opening scene which is at once visionary and political, Theseus is returning home from a conquest of the Amazons, together with his new Amazon queen, Hippolita, her beautiful young daughter, Emily, and a great company of knights. But suddenly that visionary company of ladies dressed in black appears before him, kneeling beside the highway, more or less obviously waiting for him to come by. It is indeed a vision, and one rooted in love, but it is also an omen of what is to come.

Their plight, expressed in their dress and behavior as much as by what they say, causes Theseus to stop in his tracks, and agree to attack with his army Creon, King of Thebes, who has tyrannically killed the men who were these women's lovers, husbands, and sons, and who has left their unburied bodies to be eaten by dogs. . . . After the battle Theseus has agreed to fight on their behalf, there are found, in a pile of bodies, two knights, neither fully alive nor fully dead, both of royal blood. Theseus has them sent to Athens to be kept in prison until death, since, though it would be unknightly simply to kill them outright (this is fiction, after all), it also would be dangerous to his state to allow them to go free. As V. A. Kolve has pointed out in *Chaucer and the Imagery of Narrative*,[2] in some ways prison is one of the controlling images of the tale, indeed in some ways the young knights never leave it, but are imprisoned by a love which borders on obsession, so that their love becomes a form of bondage, and gods, whether psychological, real, or planetary, impede human freedom as finally as any wall.

The two young knights of royal blood, Palamon and Arcite, are entombed beside a garden into which comes, one fine day in May, beautiful, yellow-haired young Entity, who is gathering red and white flowers, and singing like an angel. Once they have recovered from their nearly mortal wounds, they see her and are smitten. The *Knight's Tale* has begun.

Here as elsewhere, Chaucer manifests a very strong visual sense, and individual scenes, as well as individual characters, often impress themselves. The black dresses which the ladies wear point vividly not only to the many deaths which have moved them to action, but also to the sense that death is a part of life, intruding upon our moments of triumph, reminding us how short human life really is. "I tell you, we must die," they seem to be saying. Theseus, though a man of action, gets the message, and springs to the defense, almost as though it is Death itself he is going to oppose, not simply a tyrant.

But the young knights, being young, don't understand. Chancer insists that they don't, both by the naive and bitter argument they have over which of them really loves Emily (though they are both prisoners and she hardly knows that they're alive), and also by the formal symbolism present in the red and white flowers which Emily picks as she sings her May-day song. The garden through which site moves has echoes not only of Paradise, and so of the innocence which first attached to Adam and Eve, but also of the ironic and contested garden in the *Merchant's Tale*, where blindness and innocence, foolishness and insight, also play a part. But the garden in the *Knight's Tale* seems, if momentarily, transfigured. If, in a way familiar to readers of literature, its white represents (among many things) innocence, purity, and newness, its red stands for the opposite: blood, love, experience of life and the world.

Notes

1. *Death and Burial in Medieval England, 1066–1550* (London: Routledge, 1997). There are two fascinating studies of late medieval death in Michael Camille, *Master of Death: The Lifeless Art of Pierre Remiet, Illuminator* (New Haven and London: Yale University Press, 1996) and Jean-Claude Schmitt, *Ghosts in the Middle Ages: The Living*

and the Dead in Medieval Society, trans. Theresa Fagan (Chicago: University of Chicago Press, 1998).

2. *Chaucer and the Imagery of Narrative: The First Five Canterbury Tales* (Stanford, CA: Stanford University Press and London: Edward Arnold, 1984). An important book for anyone interested in the relationship of literature and art in this period. Kolve's influence has been important in this area. See further, *Speaking Images: Essays in Honor of V. A. Kolve*, ed. R. F. Yeager and Charlotte C. Morse (Asheville: Pegasus Press at The University of North Carolina at Asheville, 2001).

C. DAVID BENSON ON THE FIRST TWO TALES

Parallels between the first two tales only accentuate their differences. For example, the Knight's Tale begins with reference to Theseus, "lord," "governour," and "conquerour" (I 861–862),[25] who will be the moral hero of the tale, whereas the older man first described in Miller's Tale is the "riche gnof" John (I 3188),[26] who will be the story's dupe. A physical descent occurs near the end of each work: Arcite's tragic fall caused by the machinations of the gods is in contrast to the comic fall caused by his own gullibility that makes John an object of ridicule. The individual aesthetic of each tale illuminates that of the other. For instance, the formal set-pieces of the Knight's Tale, such as Theseus's return march from conquering the Amazons during which he encounters the Theban widows and the long, philosophical speeches exchanged by Arcite and Palamon, set a tone of pageantry and seriousness; in contrast are the more colloquial, deceptive speeches and direct action of the Miller's Tale, as when Nicholas woos Alisoun with empty love talk ("Lemman, love me, al atones, / Or I wol dyen" [I 3280–3281][27]) but more effectively and more sincerely by grabbing her hard by the hips.

The distinct styles of the first two *Canterbury Tales* can also be seen in such elements as imagery (the noble lion, tiger, even a griffin of the romance in contrast to the familiar swallow, lamb, and cat and mouse of the fabliau) and literary allusions (the classical stories and practices of the first tale

94

in contrast to more ordinary references to Cato, mystery plays, and night spells in the second). These juxtapositions do not necessarily reveal actual tellers (are we to believe that the relentless warrior is so learned or the coarse, drunken peasant so deft in using popular allusion?), but they do indicate the differing art of each tale. The texture of the tales remains distinct no matter how closely we analyze them, almost as if each were written by a separate poet. Even their vocabulary is independent: words such as *pitee*, *aventure*, and *destynee* appear frequently in the Knight's Tale but not once in the Miller's Tale, whereas the reverse is true of words such as *joly*, *derne*, and *solas*. Even overlapping vocabulary can be revealing: thus *noble*, as we might expect, is a common word in the romance, whereas its single use in the fabliau refers not to the virtue but to the coin, which describes the shiny (and mercenary?) Alisoun.

The sharp and revealing distinction between the styles of the first two tales does not mean that one is a "better" poem than the other: each is a masterpiece of its own particular kind. Reading them together, as Chaucer invites us to do by means of the Miller's intervention, reveals the specific literary achievements (and limitations) of each and begins the stylistic variety found throughout the *Canterbury Tales*. Moreover, Chaucer's spectrum of styles leads to thematic complexity. The view of world expressed in each tale is as distinct as its poetics and also equally valid. If the high seriousness and abstract philosophizing of the Knight's Tale is effectively challenged by the insistence in the Miller's Tale on the realities of both human appetite and the material physical, the latter's depiction of a society devoid of any touch of generosity and kindness is equally challenged by the former's celebration of idealism and human moral growth. As wonderful as each tale is by itself, they become greater than the sum of their parts, both aesthetically and ideologically, when read together.

Notes
25. Norton edition, p. 24, l. 3–4.
26. Norton edition, p. 77, l. 80
27. Norton edition, p. 80, l. 177–178.

Central to the *Canterbury Tales* is a larger aesthetic and philosophical question: Does human artistry impose an order on the world of experience, or does it expose a divinely created order already present within it? Tellers and tales, characters and claimants, often try to make sense of a seemingly disordered world. Forms of description, of narration, of analysis seek some way of controlling such a world—whether it be in the crazy logic of the scholars of the *Reeve's Tale*, the authoritarian despotism of the *Clerk's Tale's* Walter, the magic of the *Franklin's Tale*, or the alchemy of the *Canon's Yeoman's*. The *General Prologue* approaches the problem of organization— *ordinatio*, in the terms of late medieval bookmen—by ranging the order of the pilgrim portraits by estate: by the social class, moral condition, or profession.[19] We move from the nobility and clergy through the various professions, down through the isolates (the Wife of Bath, a widow traveling alone), the figures of agricultural exchange, to the grotesques. The portrait of the Pardoner closes the string of personal descriptions: exiled to its ending, he remains the enigma that generations of readers have seen in him. But if the Pardoner is the last of the pilgrims to be described, it is the Reeve who is the last on the journey. "And evere he rood the hyndreste of oure route" (1.622). David Wallace explains: "It seems fitting, then, that a rural watchdog should ride with everyone before him as the pilgrimage moves away from the city and into the countryside."[20] But no watchdog, rural or otherwise, can control the *Canterbury Tales*. The narrator and the Host, both of whom seek order in this welter of the classes, will be outmaneuvered by the Miller, who with his loud bagpipes, animalistic body, and wrestling skills can only barely be contained by social or by literary hierarchy.

In keeping with the orderings of power, the Knight is the one who picks the short straw and tells the first tale. "Were it by aventure, or sort, or cas, / The sothe is this: the cut fil to the Knight" (1.844–45). Was it chance, or luck, or destiny? It was of course all three, combined with the literary control of Chaucer himself. The *Canterbury Tales* begins auspiciously, but we should not take its opening at face value. No sooner has it started, than its plan is interrupted, and the fabliau confusions of the Miller quickly displace the epic assurances of the Knight. In that move lies no mere comic relief but the overarching comic purpose of the *Canterbury Tales* as a whole: a set of literary responses, challenges to social orthodoxy that reveal the fundamental inability of anyone to impose order on the world. The Host had warned the pilgrims not to be "rebel to my juggement," (1.833) but that is precisely what ensues. Words lose their meanings or take unexpected resonances; sex rears its many heads; and money emerges as the marker of both social class and literary accomplishment. What is the price we pay for literature? The first string of tales asks and answers that question in ways that define not just the Canterbury project but an idea of literary history itself.

Notes

19. See Mann, *Chaucer and Medieval Estates Satire*, and Lambdin and Lambdin, *Chaucer's Pilgrims*. For *ordinatio* and its traditions in late medieval philosophy, theology, and book production, see Parkes, "The Influence of the Concepts of *Ordinatio* and Compilatio."
20. Wallace, *Chaucerian Polity*, 155.

LEE PATTERSON ON CHAUCER AS CREATOR OF ENGLISH TRADITION

That Chaucer is the founding figure of the English literary tradition is not really in doubt. But the interesting question is not *whether* but *why*. What did Chaucer do that other poets, writing at the same time, did not? There are at least two plausible answers to this question. The first is that Chaucer was alone among his contemporaries in believing that England could develop a national literary tradition equivalent to that of the other European countries. He got this idea of a national literature primarily from the Italians, and specifically from the three great writers of the *trecento*, Dante, Petrarch, and

Boccaccio. So far as we know, Chaucer was the only person in England, and certainly the only person whose works survive who actually read the Italian writings of these three men. . . .

The most important in influence on Chaucer of the Italian tradition, however, is not individual works but rather *the idea of tradition itself*. . . .

The text in which Chaucer deals most directly with the idea of literary tradition is *The House of Fame*.[5] But *The Canterbury Tales* provided a *model* for the workings of tradition; there he showed his successors how to use one work as inspiration for another. . . .

The *Canterbury Tales* is . . . a compilation of almost every kind of writing known to the Middle Ages. Epic, romance, fabliau, saint's life, exemplum, sermon, mirror of princes, penitential treatise, tragedy, animal fable, Breton lay, confessional autobiography, Marian miracle—all these and more are present in the *Tales*. Each of the genres of which Chaucer provides an example invokes not just specific writers but a whole lexicon of different *kinds* of writing. As many of the essays presented here show, the tales are more fully understood when they are located within those literary contexts and we can understand how Chaucer is adopting—and adapting—European traditions of writing. . . .

There are twenty-four tales in all. While clearly *The Canterbury Tales* as a total project is unfinished, there are strong arguments to support the claim that Chaucer completed all of the tales (although not all of the links between tales) that he meant to write.[8] . . .

[Every] reader recognizes that the twenty-tour *Canterbury Tales* are organized according to pairs. This pattern begins with Knight–Miller, Miller–Reeve, Reeve–Cook, but then it moves into the simpler structure of in dependent pairs: Man of Law–Wife of Bath, Friar–Summoner, Clerk–Merchant, Squire–Franklin, and so on. This is not to say that there are not other patterns at work in the tales. One is the famous marriage group.[10] Another is a repeating pattern of a hagiographical tale followed by a tale of self-revelation or confession: the Man of Law followed by the Wife of Bath, the Clerk followed by the

Merchant, the Physician followed by the Pardoner, the Prioress followed by Chaucer's own tales of Sir Thopas and Melibee, and finally the Second Nun followed by the Canon's Yeoman. One can also divide the twenty-four tales into two groups of twelve, with the break coming between the Franklin's Tale and the Pardoner's Tale: the first twelve tales deal primarily with social and literary issues, the last twelve primarily with religious ones, a movement culminating in the Parson's Tale. Or the twenty-four tales can be divided into six groups of four each, following the pattern of the so-called first fragment, composed of the Knight's, Miller's, Reeve's, and Cook's tales, which is then replicated in the second group of four: Man of Law's, Wife of Bath's, Friar's, and Summoner's.[11] Regardless of the details, the primary point is that the tales are conceived as in conversation with each other: they are themselves an example of the way literary tradition works. One kind of literary form calls up another, and so on—a living and developing process in which the past provides the basis for the future, and the future casts new light upon the past.

Notes

5. *The House of Fame* (written probably in the early 1380s, prior to the completion of *Troilus and Criseyde* and before *The Canterbury Tales* project was begun) deals with the ambitions appropriate to a vernacular poet working within a European tradition dominated by Dante. The tone of the poem is satiric, but the issues are serious indeed.

8. The evidence that is most often invoked to assert that Chaucer intended to write more tales is the Host's definition of the tale-telling game in the General Prologue as requiring each pilgrim to tell two tales in either direction. But this argument ignores the fact that this is the Host's proposal, not Chaucer's. As a figure of festivity, the Host sees the journey as beginning at his tavern and then returning there, a circular pattern. But the journey is a *pilgrimage*: its goal is not a tavern but a cathedral, and the vast majority of pilgrimage narratives are one way, a linearity that implies change rather than a circularity that implies stasis. For the one-way nature of real-life medieval pilgrimage narratives, see Donald Howard, *The Idea of the Canterbury Tales* (Berkeley, Calif, 1976), pp. 29–30 and *passim*.

10. George Lyman Kittredge, "Chaucer's Discussion of Marriage," *Modern Philology* 9 (1911–1912): 435–67.

11. See Lee Patterson, *Chaucer and the Subject of History* (Madison, Wis., 1991), pp. 280–83, and *Putting the Wife in Her Place* (London, 1995), pp. 1–20.

Works by Geoffrey Chaucer

(approximate dates of composition)

The Book of the Duchess, 1368–1369

The House of Fame, 1374–1385

The Parliament of Fowles, 1380–1382

Troilus and Criseyde, 1382–1386

Legend of Good Women, 1390–1394

The Canterbury Tales, 1386–1390s

Annotated Bibliography

Ackroyd, Peter. *Chaucer*. New York: Doubleday, 2004.

This biography—one in Ackroyd's series on literary lives—is comprehensive and pleasant to read. It draws on primary sources like court records for confirmation of important dates and clues about Chaucer's personal life and employments. Much attention is given to descriptions of London life—its physical layout and ambience—as influences on the young Chaucer. Twenty-one illustrations enliven this book, including ones of Chaucer himself, scenes of the times, and illustrations from the *Tales*.

Blamires, Alcuin. *The Critics Debate: "The Canterbury Tales."* Atlantic Highlands, NJ: Humanities Press, 1987.

Students starting out in literature studies may find the literary criticism associated with Chaucer's work as daunting to navigate as the great works themselves. Specifically for Chaucer, so much commentary has been produced about the *Tales*, that beginning students might benefit from a guide through its various approaches and assumptions. This little book is that guide. The first section of the book focuses on the various approaches to reading Chaucer, the second section uses those perspectives to discuss particular tales.

Brewer, Derek. *A New Introduction to Chaucer*, second edition. London and New York: Addison Wesley Longman, 1998.

This highly readable work is especially successful at bringing Chaucer, his times and tales, alive for the reader. Brewer begins by providing a brief but memorable picture of medieval life in England during Chaucer's years. He emphasizes both the similarities between and among human beings across the centuries and the important differences. His commentary on concepts unfamiliar to the average reader—courtly love and chivalry, for example—are essential for understanding the motivations and assumptions behind each of the story-telling pilgrims.

Chesterton, G.K. *Chaucer*. New York: Greenwood Press, 1969.

Chesterton is writing here as a proud Englishman—proud of the origins of his country's literary tradition, its achievements, and its distinctive humor. There are nine essays dealing with Chaucer's life and times, Chaucer and the Renaissance, the *Canterbury Tales*, and one entitled "The Greatness of Chaucer." Throughout, Chesterton makes plain both his great esteem for Chaucer and gratitude for what Chaucer's work set in motion for the centuries that followed and those still to come.

Donaldson, E.T., ed. *Chaucer's Poetry: An Anthology for the Modern Reader*. New York: Ronald Press Company, 1958.

Donaldson is one of the prominent Chaucer scholars of this century; his book was among the best of its time and is still an excellent resource for the present generation of Chaucer readers. The author deals with the obstacle to full understanding presented by Chaucer's language by providing footnotes and translations throughout the texts. He combines clarity and scholarly straightforwardness with a keen appreciation for Chaucer that is evident throughout. This nearly thousand-page book includes sections on the *Tales*, *Troilus and Criseide*, and the minor poems; commentary about Chaucer's life, language, and pronunciation; and brief discussions about each character and tale from the *Tales*.

Donaldson, E. Talbot. *Speaking of Chaucer*. New York: W. W. Norton & Company, 1972.

Donaldson is unusually skilled at presenting learned and often complex material in lucid and entertaining form. This short collection of essays (many of them delivered as lectures while a professor of English at Yale) covers several discrete aspects of Chaucer's work, including his highly regarded essay on "Chaucer the Pilgrim" and one on everything anyone would ever want to know about the tradition of courtly love.

Fisher, John H. *The Importance of Chaucer*. Carbondale: Southern Illinois University Press, 1992.

Fisher's book is for students already familiar with Chaucer's works who want more understanding of the author's influence on literature and the English language. Individual tales and general themes are not discussed. Instead, Fisher examines what forms and subject matter constituted literature before and after Chaucer to measure the poet's influence on language and literary tradition.

George, Jodi-Anne, ed. *Geoffrey Chaucer: the General Prologue to the Canterbury Tales*. New York: Columbia University Press, 2000.

This compilation of essays and reviews on the Prologue is best-suited for students who have read the Prologue and wish to continue their Chaucer studies. The book's format follows an unusual pattern; each of the six chapters focuses on one feature of the Prologue by interweaving commentary on it by the editor with commentary made by earlier critics, including some of Chaucer's contemporaries. Topics include the use of sociology and its insights; women and feminist readings; the "new wave" of Chaucer criticism; the origins of professional readings of Chaucer; and tributes and assessments about Chaucer made by other poets and early editors. The comments of Chaucer scholar George Lyman Kittredge quoted above are among the many used and reprinted at length in this volume.

Gray, Douglas, ed. *The Oxford Companion to Chaucer*. Oxford University Press, 2003.

The dramatic expansion of Chaucer scholarship and critical commentary in the twentieth century has created a need for this compilation of topical subjects related to his life and works. It is indispensable for the advanced student doing research and also valuable as a guide for the first time reader. In alphabetical arrangement, hundreds of topics are covered: biography and history; geographical sites; cross-references from authors influential to and influenced by Chaucer; rhetorical and narration terms; concepts and traditions associated with the Middle Ages; summaries of the works, including each tale and character from *The Canterbury Tales*. The *Companion* is especially helpful for sorting out the several approaches to reading Chaucer that have generated much dispute and controversy over the years.

Hallissy, Margaret. *A Companion to Chaucer's "Canterbury Tales."* Westport, Connecticut: Greenwood Press, 1995.

Hallissy's work is explicitly written for the student new to Chaucer and medieval studies. The front piece illustration shows Chaucer reading his work to an audience—a reminder that without the invention of the printing press, oral transmission was commonplace. Hallissy gives a lively reading for each of the tales and makes helpful distinctions in the categories of pilgrims such as "Those Who Fight"; "Those Who Work"; and "Those Who Pray."

Harding, Wendy, ed. *Drama, Narrative, and Poetry in the "Canterbury Tales."* Toulouse, France: Presses Universitaires du Mirail, 2003.

This collection of essays was gathered for professors of English to prepare students for the French National Examination which requires familiarity with Chaucer's Prologue to the *Canterbury Tales*. The critics argue from the most recent approaches to Chaucerian criticism, making this a resource for more advanced students of Chaucer. Essay topics include arguments against reading the *Tales* as a drama with distinct characters and evaluations of the Wife of Bath from feminist perspectives.

Hirsh, John C. *Chaucer and the "Canterbury Tales": A Short Introduction.* Malden, MA, and Oxford: Blackwell Publishing, 2003.

Hirsh's book is for new readers of Chaucer and/or those who are eager to continue studying him. The first chapter is an especially engaging review of what is known of Chaucer's life and is followed by chapters focusing on topics like love, death, gender, class, and God. Hirsh recognizes that keeping track of all the tales is difficult so he offers a brief outline of each and one or two critical comments.

Jost, Jean E, ed. *Chaucer's Humor: Critical Essays*. New York and London: Garland Publishing, 1994.

This study of Chaucer's humor is one of a series on humor in major writers. A general approach to meanings and definitions is presented first followed by discussions of Chaucer's humor from specific perspectives, including Freudian and feminist. A third section looks closely at some of the different uses of humor in individual tales. An annotated bibliography is included to guide students interested in pursuing Chaucer studies.

Kolve, V.A., and Olsen Glending, eds. *Geoffrey Chaucer, "The Canterbury Tales": Fifteen Tales and the General Prologue*, a Norton Critical Edition. New York: W. W. Norton & Company, 2005.

This volume—one of the Norton Critical Editions—is accessible and highly informative. It features selections from the *Tales*, presented in their original Middle English with clarifying notes in the margins for unfamiliar words. Footnotes provide additional information and make for felicitous reading. Essays illuminating the background history, culture, and source materials used by Chaucer are especially helpful for students new to the poet. A small selection of notable essays in criticism concludes the book along with a chronology of Chaucer's life.

Laskaya, Anne. *Chaucer's Approach to Gender in "The Canterbury Tales."* Cambridge: D.S. Brewer (Boydell & Brewer Ltd.), 1995.

Laskaya's focus is the treatment of male and female, masculine and feminine categories in the *Tales*. A full appreciation of her erudite contribution to perspectives on Chaucer's work and in particular his treatment of medieval women requires a background in both Chaucer scholarship and feminist studies.

Lerer, Seth, ed. *The Yale Companion to Chaucer*. New Haven: Yale University Press, 2006.

Several "companions" for readers of Chaucer already exist, but the editor of this new publication recognizes the need for a collection of current and recent commentary being produced by younger scholars. In his introduction, editor Lerer explains that students in the American university system are no longer likely to have a sense of the different periods of British history and literature so this volume is designed for their benefit. Background information essential for understanding Chaucer and his times is prominently included along with analytical essays.

Patterson, Lee, ed. *Geoffrey Chaucer's The Canterbury Tales: A Casebook*. Oxford, England: Oxford University Press, 2007.

The essays in this volume are written for Chaucer readers curious about the controversies that scholars have generated over the years. Editor Patterson notes the vast volume of Chaucer commentary already available and sees a need for reformulating some of the established conclusions about Chaucer made by earlier critics that have been overlooked by younger critics eager to propose original insights.

Phillips, Helen. *An Introduction to the "Canterbury Tales": Reading, Fiction, Context*. New York: St. Martin's Press, 2000.

Although many introductory studies on Chaucer are available, this one by Helen Phillips is interested in a new reading of the *Tales*. She argues that Chaucer's worldview was not, as most scholars have concluded, politically cautious or conservative. This clearly written study assumes some prior acquaintance with Chaucer scholarship but would be appropriate for a serious beginning student as well as advanced students.

Ross, Thomas W. *Chaucer's Bawdy*. New York: E.P. Dutton & Co., 1972.

Somebody had to write this book—focused solely on Chaucer's use of ribald, obscene, and all manner of indelicate subject matter. After reading the *Tales*, one needs some help understanding—not what is so funny, or how Chaucer got away with his explicit references to body parts and functions (he did not, always), but how and where to fit witty vulgarity into large literary contexts. It is good to laugh with Chaucer; it's better to laugh and know with whom you are laughing and what tradition you are extending. Ross offers a brief discussion of these issues and argues that Chaucer's primary purpose for using bawdy language was to make his audiences laugh. The main part of the book is a glossary of three hundred risqué words in Chaucer's vocabulary. Fifteen illustrations with risqué themes taken from medieval manuscripts and paintings are also included.

Rowland, Beryl, ed. *Companion to Chaucer Studies*. Toronto, New York, London: Oxford University Press, 1968.

Books on Chaucer fill shelf after shelf after shelf in any good academic library. A beginning student would find daunting any thought of "catching up." By contrast some schools have scant resources, leaving the same student without much background, commentary, or context for any ongoing scholarship. This volume, referring to itself as another of the "companions" to reading Chaucer sets out to help students in both situations. Twenty-two chapters are offered, each on a Chaucer-related topic thought to be essential for understanding the poet by the writer of the essay.

Wilkes, G.A., and A.P. Riemer, eds. *Studies in Chaucer*. Marrickville, New South Wales: The Wentworth Press, 1981.

This series of essays on a selection of the *Tales* offered by the Department of English at the University of Sydney in Australia presumes considerable knowledge of the diverse scholarly approaches to *The Canterbury Tales*. All the citations are in Middle English, which may be confusing for the beginning student.

 Contributors

Harold Bloom is Sterling Professor of the Humanities at Yale University. He is the author of 30 books, including *Shelley's Mythmaking, The Visionary Company, Blake's Apocalypse, Yeats, A Map of Misreading, Kabbalah and Criticism, Agon: Toward a Theory of Revisionism, The American Religion, The Western Canon*, and *Omens of Millennium: The Gnosis of Angels, Dreams, and Resurrection. The Anxiety of Influence* sets forth Professor Bloom's provocative theory of the literary relationships between the great writers and their predecessors. His most recent books include *Shakespeare: The Invention of the Human*, a 1998 National Book Award finalist, *How to Read and Why, Genius: A Mosaic of One Hundred Exemplary Creative Minds, Hamlet: Poem Unlimited, Where Shall Wisdom Be Found?*, and *Jesus and Yahweh: The Names Divine*. In 1999, Professor Bloom received the prestigious American Academy of Arts and Letters Gold Medal for Criticism. He has also received the International Prize of Catalonia, the Alfonso Reyes Prize of Mexico, and the Hans Christian Andersen Bicentennial Prize of Denmark.

G.K. Chesterton was an English writer of poems, essays, and novels. Converted in 1922 to Roman Catholicism, he wrote essays promoting Catholic views. *Orthodoxy* (1959) is the most famous of his efforts.

Arthur W. Hoffman is known for his commentary on the famous opening lines of Chaucer's *General Prologue*. He is one of several prominent Chaucer scholars from an earlier generation.

E.T. Donaldson, among the most prominent of Chaucer scholars, was a professor of English at Yale. He is the author of *Speaking of Chaucer* (1970) and one of the editors of *The Norton Anthology of English Literature* (2005).

Paul G. Ruggiers used Aristotle's *Nicomachean Ethics* and *Rhetoric* to establish a vocabulary for understanding Chaucerian humor. His essay was first published in *Medieval Studies in Honor of Lillian Herlands* (1977).

V.A. Kolve is the author of *Chaucer and the Imagery of Narrative: The First Five Canterbury Tales* (1984). He has taught at Oxford and Stanford and UCLA where he is Professor of English (Emeritus).

Alcuin Blamires is Lecturer in English at St. David's University College of the University of Wales.

Winthrop Wetherbee was a professor at Cornell University in the Classics and English departments.

Anne Laskaya is Assistant Professor of English and director of the Freshman Writing Program at the University of Oregon.

Derek Brewer is Lecturer in English at the University of Cambridge. He has contributed many studies on Chaucer including *Chaucer* (First Edition 1960), *Chaucer in his Time* (1960), *Chaucer and his World* (1978), *An Introduction to Chaucer* (1984), and *A New Introduction to Chaucer* (1998).

Helen Phillips is Professor of English Studies at the University of Glamorgan.

John C. Hirsh is Professor of English at Georgetown University. In addition to his recent book on Chaucer, he has written on the medieval period of history including *The Boundaries of Faith: The Development and Transmission of Medieval Spirituality* (1996).

C. David Benson has published widely on medieval literature. He has taught at Columbia and Harvard.

Seth Lerer is Avalon Foundation Professor in Humanities and Professor of English and Comparative Literature at Stanford. In addition to editing *The Yale Companion to Chaucer*, Lerer is author of *Chaucer and His Readers: Imagining the Author in Late-Medieval England* (1993).

Lee Patterson is the author of *Chaucer and the Subject of History* (1991).

Acknowledgements

G.K. Chesterton, excerpt from "The Greatness of Chaucer" by G.K. Chesterton, from *Chaucer*: pp. 12–13, 17–20. Originally published in 1956 by Pellegrini & Cudahy. Reprinted by permission of Dorothy Collins. First Greenwood reprinting, 1969.

Arthur W. Hoffman, "Chaucer's Prologue to Pilgrimage: Two Voices." *ELH* 21:1 (1954), 1–16. © The Johns Hopkins University Press. Reprinted with permission of The Johns Hopkins University Press.

E.T. Donaldson, from *Chaucer's Poetry: An Anthology for the Modern Reader*, edited by E. Talbot Donaldson. Copyright © 1958 by Judith Anderson and Deirdre Donaldson. Used by permission of W. W. Norton & Company, Inc.

Paul G. Ruggiers, excerpt from "A Vocabulary for Chaucerian Comedy: A Preliminary Sketch," from Medieval Studies in Honor of Lillian Herlands Hornstein. Edited by Jess B. Bessinger and Robert R. Raymo. New York: New York University Press, 1976, pp. 193–225. Reprinted with permission.

V.A. Kolve, Chapter "Nature, Youth, and Nowell's Flood" by V.A. Kolve, pp. 70–71 from "Geoffrey Chaucer's The Canterbury Tales: A Casebook," edited by Pattenson, Lee (2007). Reprinted with permission from Oxford University Press.

Alcuin Blamires, *The Canterbury Tales*, 1987, Humanities Press International, reproduced with permission of Palgrave Macmillan.

Winthrop Wetherbee, excerpt from "Introduction" to *Geoffrey Chaucer: The Canterbury Tales*: pp. 10–11. © Cambridge

appearing in this volume generally appear much as they did in their original publication with few or no editorial changes. In some cases, foreign language text has been removed from the original essay. Those interested in locating the original source will find the information cited above.

Index

A

Alisoun, 94–95
Arcite, 82, 94
Aurelius, 82

B

Background of *Tales*, 19–22
Bailly, Harry
    character overview, 32–33
    competition and, 84–85
Benson, David, 94–95
Blake, William, on Wife of Bath,
    14
Blamires, Alcuin, 80–82
Boccaccio, Giovanni, 8, 78
Brewer, Derek, 87–89

C

Canon's Yeoman's Tale
    alchemy of, 96
    as nonsexual tale, 74–75
    summary of, 66
    Yeoman, character overview, 24
Carpenter, character overview, 27
Character portraits, 23–33. See
also *specific names of characters*;
tales
    Carpenter, 27
    Clerk, 26
    Cook, 27
    Doctor, 28
    Dyer, 27
    Franklin, 27
    Friar, 25
    Haberdasher, 27
    Harry Bailly, 32–33
    Knight, 23
    Man of Law, 26–27
    Manciple, 30
    Merchant, 25–26
    Miller, 30

    Monk, 24–25
    overview, 23
    Pardoner, 31–32
    Parson, 29
    Plowman, 29–30
    Prioress, 24
    Reeve, 30–31
    Seaman, 27–28
    Squire, 23–24
    Summoner, 31
    Tapestrymaker, 27
    Weaver, 27
    Wife of Bath, 28–29
    Yeoman, 24
Chaucer, Geoffrey
    attitude toward characters,
        36–39
    biographical information,
        15–18
    Bloom on, 7, 14
    as comic writer, 9–10, 21–22,
        68–69, 74–77
    Dante and, 10
    as father of English literature,
        19–20, 68, 97–100
    inspiration for *Tales*, 20
    as ironist, 73–74, 84
    as Maker, 68–70
    as narrator, 32-33, 72
    as novelist, 68
    Shakespeare and, 7–9, 13–14
    three persona in *Tales*, 35
*Chaucer and the Imagery of
    Narrative* (Kolve), 92
Chauntecleer, Bloom on, 12
Chesterton, G.K., 22, 68–70
Clerk, character overview, 26
Clerk's Tale
    authoritarian despotism in, 96
    summary of, 59–60
Coghill, Nevill, 24

Comedy, types of, 74–77
Comic writing, defined, 9–10. *See also* Humor of Chaucer
Competition in *Tales*, 84–87
Cook, character overview, 27

D
Daniell, Christopher, 91, 93n1
Dante Alighieri, 10
Death, 91–94
Death and Burial in Medieval England (Daniell), 91, 93n1
Diversity in *Tales*, 89–91
Doctor, character overview, 28
Doctor of Medicine's Tale
  competition in, 84
  summary of, 63
Donaldson, E. Talbot
  on Chaucer as comic writer, 9–10
  on Nun's Priest Tale, 12
  on the Pardoner, 11
  on Pilgrim Chaucer, 32–33
  on Prologue, 7
  on *The Tale of Sir Topaz*, 52
Dorigen, 82
Dyer, character overview, 27

E
Ellesmere Manuscript, 21
Emily, 92–93
Excess in *Tales*, 80–82

F
Fabliau genre, 78–80
Focalization, 91n3
Franklin
  character overview, 27
  personality of, 38
Franklin's Tale
  magic of, 96
  self-restraint in, 82
  summary of, 62
Friar, character overview, 25

Friar's Tale
  as nonsexual tale, 74–75
  summary of, 59

G
Gender discourse, medieval, 86
Genres present in *Tales*, 98
Griselda, 82

H
Haberdasher, character overview, 27
Hallissy, Margaret, on Bailly, 32
Hirsh, John C., 91–94
Hoffman, Arthur W., 70–72
Host. *See* Bailly, Harry
House of Fame, 98, 99n5
Humor of Chaucer
  as "comic writing," 9–10
  distinctions among comic tales and, 74–77
  greatness of, 68–69
  in the *Tales*, 21–22

I
Interpretation, diversity of, 89–91
Irony
  in Chaucer, 84
  in Monk's description, 73–74

K
Knight
  character overview, 23
  chivalric values challenged, 83
  as teller of first tale, 96–97
Knight's Tale
  competition and, 84–85
  death in, 91–94
  love in, 91–94
  lover's extravagance in, 81–82
  Miller's Tale and, 94–95
  summary of, 39–44
Kolve, V.A., 78–80, 92

L

Laskaya, Anne, 84
Lerer, Seth, 96–97

M

Man of Law
    character overview, 26–27
    self-importance deflated, 37
    vacillating attitude toward
        Providence and, 83
Man of Law's Tale
    poverty and, 91
    summary of, 49–50
Manciple, character overview, 30
Manciple's Tale, summary of, 66–67
Marlowe, Christopher, 8
Melibee, Tale of, summary of, 52–53
Merchant, character overview, 25–26
Merchant's Tale
    in fabliau genre, 79
    garden in, 93
    as sexual tale, 74–75, 76
    summary of, 61
Miller
    character overview, 30
    fabliau confusions of, 97
    wart and, 36–37
Miller's Tale
    antifeminist nature of, 89
    competition in, 84
    in fabliau genre, 79
    Knight's Tale and, 94–95
    plot of, 87–88
    as sexual tale, 74–75, 76
    summary of, 44–47
    vulgarity in, 90–91
Monk
    character overview, 24–25
    irony in description of, 73–74
Monk's Tale, summary of, 53
Moralities, conflicting, 89–91
Mortality rates, Medieval, 91–92

N

Number of tales, 98, 99n8
Nun's Priest Tale
    competition in, 84
    Donaldson on, 12
    summary of, 53–55

O

Ockham's razor, 83
Order, absence of, 82–84, 96–97

P

Pardoner
    blasphemy of, 83
    Bloom on, 7, 9
    character overview, 31–32
    Donaldson on, 10
    as enigma, 96
    excess and, 80–81
    intolerance of Christian society
        and, 83–84
Pardoner's Tale
    as nonsexual tale, 74–75, 76
    summary of, 63–65
Parson, character overview, 29
Parson's Tale, summary of, 67
Patterson, Lee, 19–20, 97–100
Peasant's Revolution of 1381, 21
Phillips, Helen, 89–91
Philosophical questions, 96–97
Physician's Tale, see *Doctor of
    Medicine's Tale*
Plowman, character overview,
    29–30
Political stance, 90
Polyphonic text, 89–90
Portraits, character. *See* Character
    portraits
Prioress
    character overview, 24
    table manners of, 36–37
Prioress's Tale, summary of, 50–51
Prologue
    opening lines of, 70–72

organization of, 96–97
precise portraiture in, 7, 34
Puns, 22

R
Reeve, character overview, 30–31
Reeve's Tale
   in fabliau genre, 79
   logic of scholars in, 96
   as sexual tale, 74–75
   summary of, 47–48
Restraint in *Tales*, 80–82
Rime of Sir Topas, 69, 73
Ross, Thomas W., 22
Ruggiers, Paul G., 74–78

S
Seaman, character overview, 27–28
Second Nun's Tale, summary of, 62
Sexual tales, 74–76
Shakespeare, William, and
   Chaucer, 7–9, 13–14
Shipman's Tale, 74–75
Shipman's Tale
   in fabliau genre, 79
   as sexual tale, 74–75, 76
Shipman's Tale, summary of, 50
Sir Topaz, Tale of, summary of, 51–52
Sources, 78, 97
Speght, Thomas, 19
Squire, character overview, 23–24
Squire's Tale, summary of, 62
Structure of *Tales*, 98–99
Summoner, character overview, 31
Summoner's Tale
   as nonsexual tale, 74–75
   summary of, 59

Summoner's Tale, in fabliau genre,
   79

T
Tale of Melibee, summary of, 52–53
Tale of Sir Topaz, summary of,
   51–52
Tapestrymaker, character overview,
   27
Theseus, 83, 92–93, 94
Troilus and Criseyde, as Chaucer's
   masterpiece, 21–22

V
Variety in *Tales*, 89–91

W
Weaver, character overview, 27
Wetherbee, Winthrop, 82–84
Wife of Bath
   Blake on, 14
   Bloom on, 7, 9, 10
   character overview, 28–29
   Donaldson on, 13–14
   excess and, 80–81
   personality of, 37
   self-awareness of, 83
Wife of Bath's Tale
   poverty and, 91
   summary of, 55–58
William of Ockham, 83
Women, 21, 86–87, 88–89

Y
Yeoman, character overview, 24